PATTERNS OF REPRODUCTION
OF FOUR SPECIES OF VESPERTILIONID BATS
IN PARAGUAY

PATTERNS OF REPRODUCTION
OF FOUR SPECIES OF VESPERTILIONID BATS
IN PARAGUAY

BY

PHILIP MYERS

UNIVERSITY OF CALIFORNIA PRESS
BERKELEY · LOS ANGELES · LONDON

UNIVERSITY OF CALIFORNIA PUBLICATIONS IN ZOOLOGY

Volume 107
Approved for publication January 16, 1976
Issued January 14, 1977

UNIVERSITY OF CALIFORNIA PRESS
BERKELEY AND LOS ANGELES
CALIFORNIA

UNIVERSITY OF CALIFORNIA PRESS, LTD.
LONDON, ENGLAND

ISBN: 0-520-09554-5
LIBRARY OF CONGRESS CATALOG CARD NUMBER: 76-3878
©1977 BY THE REGENTS OF THE UNIVERSITY OF CALIFORNIA
PRINTED IN THE UNITED STATES OF AMERICA

CONTENTS

Introduction 1
Study Area 2
    Chaco 4
    Región Oriental 7
Methods 8
Patterns of Reproduction
    Lasiurus ega females 11
    Lasiurus ega males 13
    Eptesicus furinalis females 16
    Eptesicus furinalis males 18
    Myotis albescens females 20
    Myotis albescens males 22
    Myotis nigricans females 23
    Myotis nigricans males 24
Temperature and activity 25
Aggregations of *Myotis nigricans* and *Myotis albescens* 27
Discussion
    Patterns of breeding 28
    Storage of spermatozoa 31
    Interstitial tissue 32
    Post partum estrus 33
    Age at first breeding 33
    Population structure 33
    Social aggregations 34
    Comparisons of reproductive patterns 35
Summary 36
Acknowledgments 37
Literature Cited 38

PATTERNS OF REPRODUCTION OF FOUR SPECIES OF VESPERTILIONID BATS IN PARAGUAY

by

PHILIP MYERS[*]

(A contribution from the Museum of Vertebrate Zoology
of the University of California, Berkeley)

INTRODUCTION

The diversity of breeding patterns of bats suggests that their reproductive patterns are unusually sensitive to environmental change. Modifications of litter size, number of litters per year, timing of breeding, and the amount of energy going into related activities, have been recorded and may be correlated with changes in environmental conditions. Bats may meet shifting conditions by phenotypic modifications of individual breeding patterns, or by long-term evolutionary adaptation. Studies comparing populations of one species (or of closely related species) reproducing under different environmental conditions are the primary source of information concerning both types of response, and are important in elucidating the adaptive significance of modifications of breeding patterns. This study presents an examination of the biology of reproduction of four species of vespertilionid bats in Paraguay, South America, and a comparison with related bats in other parts of the world.

The evolutionary centers of most families of bats are in the tropics (Koopman, 1970), and all families have many species in the tropical zones. Here, where seasonal fluctuations in climate are often reduced, aseasonality in breeding might be expected. Such occurs in a few cases (*e.g.*, Wimsatt and Trapido, 1952; Tamsitt and Valdivieso, 1965a,b; Marshall and Corbet, 1959), but in many others breeding seasons are strongly restricted or there are sharply defined seasons when no breeding takes place (*e.g.*, Baker and Bird, 1936; Gopalakrishna, 1947; Anderson and Wimsatt, 1963; Wilson and Findley, 1970, 1971; Medway, 1971). The time of year when breeding occurs may vary geographically, corresponding to variations in the time when certain resources are available (Dwyer, 1970b; Fleming, Hooper, and Wilson, 1972). Cases of delayed implantation (Mutere, 1967) and delayed development (Fleming, 1971) are also known from tropical populations. The gestation period of some tropical bats is unusually long for animals of such small body size (Wimsatt and Trapido, 1952; Mitchell, 1965). Thus, despite the reduced seasonality of the climate, special patterns of reproduction are found in populations of bats in the tropics.

Only the Vespertilionidae, Rhinolophidae, and Molossidae are well represented in temperate regions, though the ranges of species of a few other families also extend into the temperate zone. The use of temperate habitats has been accompanied by further modifications of the breeding schedules of tropical bats in most populations examined. All north temperate populations of bats whose reproduction has been studied breed once a year (see Asdell, 1964; or Carter, 1970, for reviews). Most further modify their breeding by altering the time relationships between gametogenesis, copulation, ovulation, implantation, and parturition. These modifications include a delay between implantation and parturition ("delayed development," Bradshaw, 1962), a delay between ovulation and implantation ("delayed implantation," Courrier, 1927; Planel *et al.*, 1962; Peyre and Herlant, 1963), or a delay between copulation and ovulation ("storage of spermatozoa," first described by Pagenstecher, 1859).

[*]Present address: Museum of Zoology, University of Michigan, Ann Arbor, Michigan 48109, USA.

Further, some bats migrate to areas that provide suitable conditions during the winter. Both short distance (*e.g.*, altitudinal migrations or migrations to hibernacula) and long distance migrations are known (see Griffin, 1970, for review).

Storage of spermatozoa by females of the Vespertilionidae and Rhinolophidae is the best known and most widespread of these patterns in north temperate regions (Guthrie, 1933; Wimsatt, 1942, 1944; Sluiter and Bowman, 1951; Pearson *et al.*, 1952; Orr, 1954; and others). Storage of spermatozoa has always been associated with hibernation; in fact, it has been suggested that the relationship is obligatory (Wimsatt, 1960; McNab, 1974). Wimsatt (1960) further suggests that the maintenance of enlarged male accessory glands (which remain large after the involution of the interstitial tissue), and continued copulatory behavior, also depend on hibernation.

Many species of vespertilionids are widely distributed and encounter a broad range of environmental conditions. Surprisingly few studies take advantage of this to investigate plasticity of breeding patterns, or to attempt to determine the aspects of their environment most important to the breeding of bats. The few studies dealing with these questions have revealed that variability in breeding patterns exists, even among populations of a single species, and suggest that these variations may sometimes be correlated with regional differences in factors such as temperature and availability of food (see Courrier, 1927; Baker and Bird, 1936; Dwyer, 1963a,b, 1968; and Medway, 1971, for *Miniopterus*; Wilson and Findley, 1970, 1971, for *Myotis*; Fleming, *et al.*, 1972, for miscellaneous phyllostomatids; and Mutere, 1973, for *Otomops*).

The present study reports on an investigation of the reproductive biology of four species of vespertilionid bats in Paraguay (in subtropical to temperate South America). The object is to describe reproductive patterns in detail, compare them with the patterns of related species, and, if possible, suggest which aspects of the environment are important in their determination.

The species examined are *Lasiurus ega* (Gervais), *Eptesicus furinalis* (D'Orbigny), *Myotis albescens* (E. Geoffroy), and *M. nigricans* (Schinz). Both species of *Myotis* range from northern Central America into Argentina (from the tropics to temperate South America), and for *M. nigricans*, detailed reproductive data are available from one tropical locality. *Lasiurus ega* ranges from the southwestern United States to northern Argentina (Hall and Kelson, 1959; Cabrera, 1957). While no intensive study of this species has been made, its congeners in the United States and Canada, *L. borealis* and *L. cinereus,* store spermatozoa and migrate. Members of the genus *Lasiurus* are solitary, tree-roosting bats, in contrast to the numerous species of *Myotis* and *Eptesicus*, which tend to be colonial. Members of the genus *Eptesicus* range from Canada to Argentina. The pattern of reproduction of *Eptesicus fuscus* in the United States is well known, and involves hibernation and storage of spermatozoa by females. Neither *Eptesicus* nor *Lasiurus* has been studied in the tropics.

STUDY AREA

Paraguay, a country approximately the size of California, is subdivided into two major physiographic regions. The Chaco lies to the west of the Río Paraguay; the Región Oriental (= Eastern Region) lies to the east (fig. 1). Field work with *Myotis*, and about half of the work with *Eptesicus* and *Lasiurus*, was done in the Chaco between latitudes 22° and 24°S. The rest of the work with *Eptesicus* and *Lasiurus* was done in the Eastern Region near Asunción, latitude 25°S. Most of the Chaco portion of the study was carried out at

Fig. 1. Paraguay: Physiographic zones and study area.

Rincón Charrua (23°20′S latitude, 59°5′longitude), a ranch located 270 km NW of Villa Hayes on the Trans-Chaco Highway, on the northwest border of Departamento Presidente Hayes. Some specimens of *Myotis* came from neighboring ranches (Buen Amigo, Juan de Zalazar, Siete Horizontes, Ca-í, and an experimental station of the Ministerio de Agricultura y Ganaderia), all within a 50 km radius of Rincón Charrua. The following description of Chaco habitat is restricted primarily to the zone in which most bats were taken.

Chaco

The Paraguayan Chaco, comprising 60% of the land mass of Paraguay, is part of a great plain that also extends into southeastern Bolivia and northern Argentina. Despite this geographic prominence, fewer than 4% of Paraguay's 2.3 million people live within its limits (Bertoni and Gorham, 1973). Houses and other man-made structures, common roosts for bats, are a relatively recent and still scarce feature of the landscape. The land is flat; rock outcroppings or caves are not available as roost sites. Free surface water is present in the form of a few sluggish rivers and lakes, but much of this water is too saline for consumption by humans or livestock. The soil is shallow and composed of fine alluvial clay overlying saline sand. Cattle ranchers have bulldozed shallow depressions in the nearly impermeable clay; these fill with rain water during the wet season and in some areas remain filled all year. The concentrations of birds and mammals (including bats) around these ponds during the dry season attests their importance to wildlife.

Climate. — There are clines of decreasing annual rainfall and increasing temperature from southeast to northwest. On the Río Paraguay, the average annual rainfall is about 1400 mm, and the mean annual temperature is 24°C. At the Bolivian border in the north-

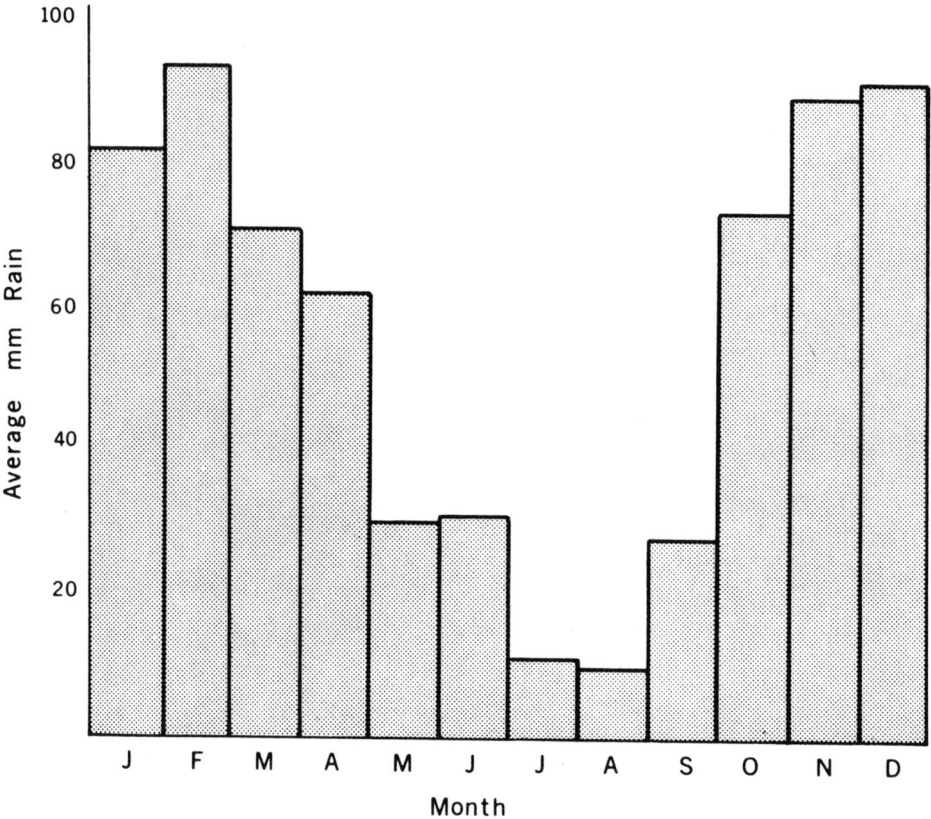

Fig. 2. Mean monthly rainfall at Km 160, Paraguayan Chaco, for 1942-1966. (Data from Gorham, 1973)

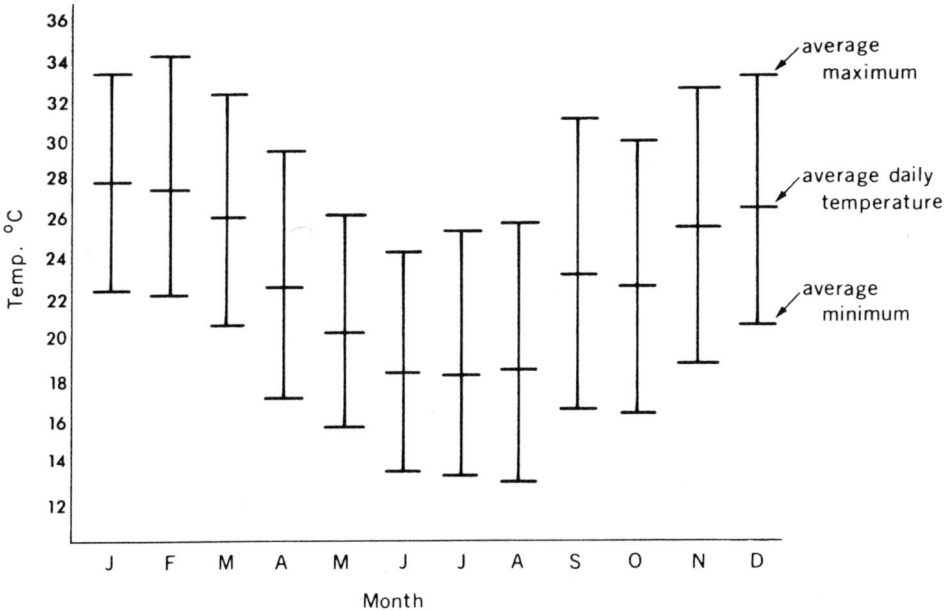

Fig. 3. Average monthly temperature at Pozo Colorado, Paraguayan Chaco, for 1971-1973.

west, annual rainfall is 300 mm and the mean annual temperature is 26°C. Rincón Charrua receives an average of 900 to 1000 mm of rain annually (data from Gorham, 1973; Sánchez, 1973). Strong seasonal differences in rainfall and temperature are apparent (figs. 2 and 3). The summer months, October through March, are hot and wet, while the winter months, April through September, tend to be cool and dry. The data presented in fig. 2 are 25 year averages of rainfall at Km 160, approximately 150 km north of Rincón Charrua, and the data in fig. 3 are 2-3 year averages from Pozo Colorado, a military base about 20 km southeast of Rincón Charrua. The coldest months at Pozo Colorado are June-August, when the average daily minimum for the years 1970-1973 was 13°C. Temperatures fall below freezing several times each winter, and may do so in any month from May to September. However, temperatures colder than 5°C are experienced on fewer than 10% of the nights during the winter, and cold nights are often accompanied by warm days. The average daily maximum in June, for example, is over 24°C. Although there tends to be a large variation from year to year, statistics from the Mennonite colonies and older military bases 100-200 km to the northwest suggest that these averages are fairly typical (Gorham, 1973).

One important aspect of the climate not apparent from these averages is the seasonal change in weather pattern. The summer months are very hot and rain falls in brief, intense thunderstorms. During a two week collecting period in late January, 1973, for example, temperatures below 35°C were never recorded except during brief showers. In the winter, cold fronts of antarctic origin alternate with northern tropical weather fronts. The southern storms bring cold, overcast weather and drizzle that may last several days. After the rain, there are usually a few days of cold clear weather followed by warming as the influence of a tropical front is felt. Before the next cold front arrives, maximum daily temperatures may exceed 30°C. This winter pattern further results in abrupt change in temperature

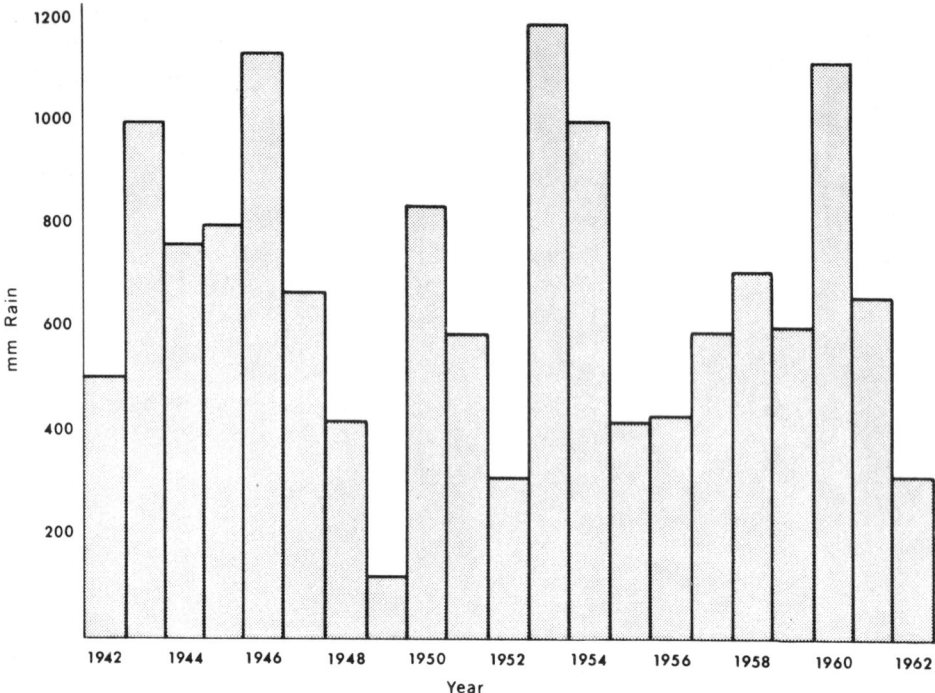

Fig. 4. Yearly rainfall at Km 160, Paraguayan Chaco, for 1942-1962. (Data from Gorham, 1973)

when cold fronts arrive. I experienced several changes of over 20°C in a few hours, and changes of over 30°C are on record. Also, while winter rains are widespread, summer rains are very local, and most water accumulates where it falls rather than being distributed by rivers. Therefore, one area may experience extensive flooding while a few miles away drought prevails.

An equally important aspect of the climate is its variability from year to year (fig. 4). Droughts lasting several months are common. The onset of the rainy season and the arrival of the first winter cold fronts may vary by more than two months in successive years (Gorham, 1973). That this variation can be biologically critical was demonstrated by the death of dozens of migratory swallows when a late cold front arrived in October, 1972. Unfortunately, the recording of weather data has been initiated relatively recently in most parts of Paraguay, and data to adequately document this type of variation are lacking.

Vegetation. – In the zone of this study there are two predominant plant communities. The first is grassland ("Pantanal" of Short, 1975), often associated with stands of caranday palms (*Copernicia* spp.) (plate 1a). Dense bunch grasses predominate and few forbs are present. These grasslands often flood to a depth of several inches during the wet season. Ranchers usually burn the grassland annually, believing that this practice improves the quality of the range. The combination of burning and flooding probably limits the diversity of the plant and animal communities. There are normally few vertebrates in the grasslands except near the forest edge (which neither burns nor floods). Grassland is the most suitable habitat for ranching in Paraguay, and is extensively grazed by cattle and horses.

The second vegetation type is thorn forest (plate 1b), which occurs on slightly elevated islands in the grassland near the Río Paraguay ("Algarrobo-Quebracho-Palo Santo Woodlands" of Short, 1975). To the northwest, the islands become larger and eventually coalesce to form nearly continuous forest. The trees are low, seldom exceeding 10 m except in gallery forest along rivers. Species of *Prosopis* predominate. Also present are species of *Schinopsis, Tabebuia, Zizyphus, Diospyros, Aspidosperma, Caesalpinia, Bulnesia sarmientii,* and others (Adamoli *et al.*, 1972; Short, 1975). There may be a ground cover including cacti (*Cereus coryne, C. validos, Opuntia quimile,* and others) and spiny bromeliads (*Bromelia hieronymi*). The result is often a very dense, even impenetrable, forest (plate 2a), and local variations in density and species composition are pronounced.

Most plants flower in the winter and spring in the Chaco, although no month is completely without flowers on some trees or herbs. In this study, frugivorous birds (*e.g.*, trogons and toucans) and bats (*Artibeus*) were seen in the Chaco only in the winter. Most birds breed beginning in the spring (September) in Paraguay (personal observation). Available breeding records for mammals are scanty but indicate that in the Chaco most rodents are pregnant in the spring and fall. Gestation in bats, as will be seen, takes place during the spring and summer months (September through February).

Rincón Charrua, a ranch of about 20,000 hectares, is approximately 60% forested according to the owner. Juan de Zalazar, covering 110,000 ha., is approximately 12.5% grassland (Wetzel and Lovett, 1974). All of the bats handled came from forested areas or from areas very close to forest. One species, *Lasiurus ega*, was most commonly collected at ponds near extensive stands of caranday palms.

The following species of bats were captured at or near Rincón Charrua: *Noctilio leporinus, N. labialis, Artibeus lituratus, A. planirostris, Desmodus rotundus, Myotis albescens, M. nigricans, M. simus, M. riparius, Eptesicus furinalis, Lasiurus borealis, L. ega, Molossops planirostris, M. temmincki, M. brachymeles, Eumops glaucinus, E. bonariensis, Promops occultus, Molossus molossus, M. ater.*

Región Oriental

Asunción, the capital of Paraguay, is located on the east bank of the Río Paraguay. It is within a few miles of the eastern border of the Chaco, yet the transition from Chaco to Región Oriental is as abrupt biologically and geologically as it is politically. Most of my work in the Región Oriental was done within 50 km of Asunción, and the majority was done within the city limits. Therefore, my descriptions of the Eastern Region will be limited to the Paraguay River valley.

The Paraguay River valley is a plain crossed by a few lines of low hills (plate 2b). The soils are complex and varied, but generally much more permeable and less saline than in the Chaco. There are numerous rivers and considerable topographic relief. The hills are rocky, and shallow caves are present. Water lies near the surface and is potable; as a result, most ranches have wells. The human population density is much greater than in the Chaco. Caves, wells and houses are often used by bats as roosts.

Weather records are available for over 30 years for Asunción. The weather pattern is similar to that of the Chaco, but is more moderate. Rainfall, temperature, and insolation are distributed seasonally approximately as they are at Pozo Colorado (figs. 2-4).

As in the Chaco, the vegetation of the Paraguay River valley includes grassland and forest, but the species present differ and the species diversity appears to be much greater. The forest is higher, less dense, and usually less thorny than that of the Chaco. Epiphytes are more abundant, but the trees are not so impressively tall and diverse as in true rainforest (which occurs in Paraguay only along the Río Paraná). Whether this difference is due to natural conditions or human interference is unknown, as the area around Asunción has been under intense cultivation for over 400 years. Grasslands are composed predominantly of bunch grasses, and more species of grasses and forbs are present than in the Chaco. Flooding is less widespread but, as in the Chaco, the grassland is burned annually.

Flowering appears to be less seasonally restricted in the Región Oriental than in the Chaco. Breeding patterns of birds and rodents are similar to Chaco patterns, but more individuals breed during the winter (personal observations). Pregnant rodents were captured during most months. Fruit-eating birds and bats are abundant; indeed, members of the Phyllostomatidae were the most frequently captured bats in the Eastern Region.

Species of bats captured in the Región Oriental include the following: *Noctilio leporinus, N. labialis, Tonatia sylvicola, Chrotopterus auritus, Glossophaga soricina, Carollia perspicillata, Sturnira lilium, Vampyrops lineatus, Artibeus lituratus, A. planirostris, A.* sp., *Pygoderma bilabiatum, Desmodus rotundus, Myotis nigricans, Eptesicus furinalis, Lasiurus ega, L. borealis, Molossops brachymeles, M. planirostris, M. temmincki, Eumops auripendulus major, E. bonariensis, Promops occultus, Molossus molossus, M. ater, Tadarida brasiliensis, T. laticaudata.*

Abundance of insects. – Changes in the abundance of insects might be expected to have a profound effect on the biology of insectivorous bats. The effect of changes in weather on insect populations in both the Chaco and Región Oriental is striking. One of the most memorable features of Chaco zoology is the mosquito population, which, with those of other flying insects, follows definite cycles. During the winter, mosquitoes are ubiquitous but relatively inactive, especially when the temperature is low. During the summer, the number of flying mosquitoes increases dramatically following a rain. Subsequently, as the temperature of the air and of the standing water rises, mosquito activity decreases until virtually none is seen. Within a few weeks, rain falls and the cycle repeats. Thus, for an animal feeding on mosquitoes during the summer, food is abundant temporarily, but subsequently scarce for days or weeks. It is my strong subjective impression that the activity of other nocturnal flying insects follows a similar pattern.

In the Región Oriental, changes in insect abundance are less striking. Mosquitoes, for example, rarely reach the concentrations seen in the Chaco, nor do they ever become as scarce. It is probable that the milder climate, combined with the greater diversity of habitats, and the more continuous flowering and fruiting by plants, result in insects being available more continuously to predators.

METHODS

Field procedures. – Field facilities in Paraguay are limited, and the difficulties associated with a sampling program are sometimes severe. All unpaved roads (including the Trans-Chaco Highway) are closed when their surfaces are wet. Weather permitting, I visited ranches with known bat roosts in the central Chaco at least once a month during the period October, 1972 - December, 1973. During these visits I was a guest of the owner of the ranch and invariably enjoyed the full cooperation of his employees. In the interval between visits, however, I had no assurance that ranch personnel would not disturb animals roosting in buildings; disturbance certainly occurred in several instances.

Bats were captured by mist nets or by hand. *Myotis nigricans* and *M. albescens* were usually obtained from roosts of two types, which they shared with species of *Molossops, Eumops,* and *Molossus*. The first type is in buildings, usually where the ridge pole of the roof meets the wall. Here both species of *Myotis* are found with *Molossus* and *Molossops* in clusters of hundreds or thousands of individuals. They are reluctant to fly and are relatively easy to capture. Hollows in walls, or other narrow, dark interstices are also utilized. The second type of roost occurs in houses with roofs made of split palm logs (plate 3a). The logs, usually 9-10 ft long, are slightly hollowed and placed on the roof so that their edges overlap. Bats roost between the logs.

Lasiurus and *Eptesicus* were captured by setting mist nets over water. Swimming pools in Asunción and artificial cattle ponds in the Chaco were the most reliable sources. Up to 20 or 30 individuals of a species might be caught in an evening, although usually many hours of netting produced few bats. One small *Eptesicus* roost, containing fewer than 10 bats, was found between two beams in a porch in Asunción. Only one roosting *Lasiurus ega* was discovered, a torpid individual hanging in a clump of leaves in a mango tree.

Whenever possible, I obtained a monthly sample of at least 10 females and 5 males of each species (table 1). Male and female reproductive tracts were removed from recently killed bats and preserved in Bouin's solution, which was later replaced with 70% ethanol. In the field, I measured the length of the testes and male accessory glands (from the base of the bladder to their most anterior projection), and recorded whether the tubules of the

TABLE 1

Size of Monthly Samples of Bats

	Lasiurus ega ♂	*Lasiurus ega* ♀	*Eptesicus furinalis* ♂	*Eptesicus furinalis* ♀	*Myotis nigricans* ♂	*Myotis nigricans* ♀	*Myotis albescens* ♂	*Myotis albescens* ♀
Jan.	2	2	0	13	2	4	4	0
Feb.	7	3	4	1	1	3	8	6
March	4	3	2	2	1	1	5	0
April	7	7	7	4	7	10	5	10
May	2	3	1	2	1	2	6	10
June	0	0	0	2	5	10	5	10
July	7	1	2	4	8	15	5	12
Aug.	12	11	2	3	1	11	2	17
Sept.	10	18	6	19	5	8	11	11
Oct.	7	7	7	18	5	7	4	6
Nov.	1	2	0	8	6	12	9	16
Dec.	1	5	4	5	0	3	3	9

epididymis were visible macroscopically. I noted the condition of the nipples, vagina (open or closed), and pubic symphysis (relaxed or closed) for females. When pregnancies occurred, I recorded the number, position, and crown-rump length of the embryo(s). Follicles and corpora lutea are not visible to the naked eye.

Several hundred bats were marked by tattooing and released. I used a Pet Tattoo "Registrar's Outfit," from Weston Mfg. and Supply, to place numbers on the right wing between the fifth finger and body (Bonaccorso and Smythe, 1972). Initially I marked and released a fraction of all species caught in localities to which I knew I would return. After 6 months with recaptures of no *Lasiurus*, and of few *Eptesicus*, I stopped marking these species. Tattooed *Myotis*, on the other hand, were frequently recaptured. The high recapture rate of *Myotis* is undoubtedly due to the fact that they were caught at their roost and had less opportunity to escape. The high recapture rate further indicates that tattooing does little harm to the bats.

Laboratory procedures. – Fluid-preserved testes from male *Eptesicus* and *Lasiurus* were measured under a dissecting microscope and were weighed (wet) to the nearest 0.1 mg. Unfortunately this was not done for most *Myotis* males, and only field measurements of length are available. Volumes of *Myotis* testes were calculated using the formula for a prolate spheroid ($V = 0.523$ length X width^2) (Lidicker, 1973). The Pearson's correlation coefficient between the weights and volumes of seven *Myotis* testes was $r = .996$.

Male and female reproductive tracts were imbedded in Paraplast, sectioned at 10 μ, stained with Ehrlich's hematoxylin, and counterstained with eosin Y. Female tracts were serially sectioned. Male tracts were examined and relative abundance of cells in different stages of spermatogenesis, presence or absence of spermatozoa in the epididymides, and relative size of the lumina of the seminiferous tubules and tubules of the epididymis were recorded. I estimated the volume occupied by interstitial cells by superimposing a grid of 100 dots over a series of sections and recorded the number of dots touching interstitial cells. The percentage of "hits" is equal to the percentage of testis volume occupied by interstitial cells (Weibel *et al.*, 1966). Sectioned ovaries were examined for morphological differences among species and to determine what seasonal changes occur within a species. The uteri of non-pregnant females were searched for spermatozoa.

Age determination. – Very young bats were recognized by their small size and distinct pelage. The phalangeal epiphyses do not fuse completely until the bats are about 3 to 4 months old (Wilson and Findley, 1971). Unfused phalanges are usually easily detected on dry skins. I found, however, that X-rays of the phalanges examined under a dissecting microscope, revealed that the phalanges of several bats, which otherwise would have been classified as fused, were actually unfused. Furthermore, in some individuals the centra of the tail vertebrae do not fuse until after the phalanges. Using these criteria bats were placed in two age categories, mature and immature. The exact age at which a young bat is classed as "mature" is unknown, but is believed to be approximately 4 months.

Identification. – Large series of *Myotis nigricans* and *M. albescens* were obtained. Some individuals, particularly immature bats, were difficult to assign to one species or the other. A stepwise discriminant function analysis (BMD Program, Version of Sept. 1, 1965, Health Sciences Computing Facility, UCLA; Berkeley FSU-Cal Version, 11/27/68) was used to facilitate identification of these individuals. The characters suggested by LaVal (1973) were used in the analysis.

PATTERNS OF REPRODUCTION

Lasiurus ega females

Seasonal pattern (fig. 5). — In the Región Oriental breeding begins in the fall (May), when females were first found to have spermatozoa in their uteri. The time of ovulation may vary geographically. Eastern females with tubal ova and fresh corpora lutea were first found in mid-August, approximately three months after initial copulations. Females from the Chaco from the same period had not ovulated, although their ovaries contained very large follicles, and pregnancies were first found in the Chaco in mid-September. Because no individuals of *Lasiurus* were collected in the Chaco from May through July, it is not known whether the start of copulation shifts comparably. The duration of pregnancy is from 3 to 3½ months, and young are born in the spring (late November or early December). Female *Lasiurus* from the Eastern Region may give birth earlier than females from the Chaco, but evidence for this is inconclusive. There is only one breeding season. The average number of embryos for 17 pregnant females was 2.9; the mode, 3; the range, 2-4.

Anatomy (table 2). — The cornua of the uteri of female *Lasiurus* are approximately equal in size, 2 mm long X 1 mm diameter in nonpregnant, parous individuals. In cross section the ovaries are round or slightly oval, and about 1 mm in diameter. Among the four species studied, *Lasiurus* females are remarkable for their large rete and prominent epoöphoron tubules. The ova of *Lasiurus* are unusual in that they often contain one or more dark-

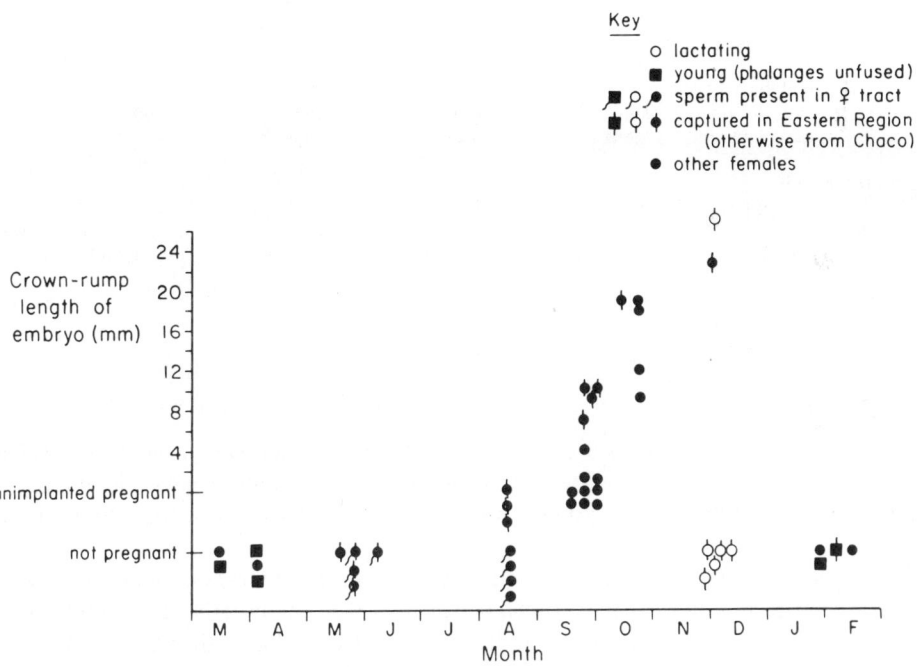

Fig. 5. Annual breeding pattern of female *Lasiurus ega*. Only females whose ovaries were examined microscopically, or which were pregnant, are represented.

TABLE 2*

Anatomy of Female Reproductive Tracts

	Myotis albescens	Myotis nigricans	Lasiurus ega	Eptesicus furinalis
Bursa ovarica	complete	complete	complete	complete
Orifice	medium slit	medium slit	tiny	tiny
Epoöphoron	small-medium	small	prominent	small-medium
Ovary				
Location	pelvic	pelvic	pelvic	pelvic
Shape	ellipsoidal	ellipsoidal	ellipsoidal	ellipsoidal
Lobes	0	0	0	0
Fissures	0	0	0	0
Tunica albuginea	thin-medium	thin	thin	thin-medium
Rete	medium-large	medium-large	prominent	medium
Ripe follicles				
No. & (litter size)	1? (1)	1 (1)	3-4 (3-4)	3-5 (1); ?(1)**
Diameter (mm)	0.4 mm	.33 mm+	0.3-0.4 mm	0.3 mm+
Antrum	small	small	small	small
Thecal gland	thin-medium	thin	medium-thin	thin
Interstitial gland type				
Thecal	some	much	much	some
Stromal	much	much	much ?	much
Medullary cord	?	?	?	–
Gonadal adrenal				
in cortex	–	–	?	–
in medulla	–	–	?	–
at epoöphoron	some	some	some ?	some ?
accessory adrenal	some	some	some	some
Luteal glands				
No. of cell types	1	1	1	1
Accessory corpora	0	0	0	yes (1st breeding)
Persistence	early lactation	late preg.- early lact.	into lactation	into lactation

*After Mossman and Duke, 1973.
**First breeding period; 2nd b. p.

staining inclusions of irregular size and shape, and of unknown origin or significance (plate 4). The inclusions are not found in ripe ova nor in preimplantation stages of developing embryos, in contrast to the "crystalline structures" found in the ova of *Macrotus californicus* females (Bleier, 1975).

Follicles. – In mid-May, when copulation first occurs, most females examined possessed five to ten tertiary follicles of about 260 μ diameter (plate 4). By early July the three to four follicles which will be ovulated are slightly larger (up to 280 μ) than the remainder. In August, just prior to ovulation, their diameter exceeds 300 μ. At this time numerous tertiary follicles of up to 300 μ diameter are conspicuous; they will persist for a few weeks after ovulation before undergoing atresia. Polyovular follicles, commonly found in the ovaries of young of some mammals, were seen in two mature individuals (one follicle in each instance).

Corpora lutea. — Newly formed corpora lutea, from females with unimplanted morulae or blastocysts, range in diameter from 330 μ to 630 μ (fig. 6a). New corpora are extensively vascularized; large vessels develop inside the corpus soon after it forms (plate 4). The border of the corpus is distinct and paraluteal cells are present but uncommon. The nuclei are swollen, and faint nucleoli are present. Corpora from females in mid-pregnancy are similar, but the diameter of the corpus decreases slightly and the nucleoli become very prominent. Vascularity changes little. During late pregnancy and early lactation the diameter of the corpus luteum continues to decrease gradually, and during lactation the corpus disappears completely. Vascularity gradually decreases, the nuclei shrivel, and the nucleoli disappear (plate 4).

At no time during the history of the corpus luteum of a female *Lasiurus* does it equal the maximum size of the mature corpus of female *Myotis* (greater than 700 μ), nor does it contain as many cells (figs. 6a, c, d). Pregnant female *Lasiurus* usually have two to four corpora (equal to the number of embryos), while one corpus luteum is the rule for female *Myotis*. There is no abrupt change in the size and morphology of the corpus such as is suggested for female *Myotis* during mid-pregnancy (see below).

Young. — No tracts from young females of this species were sectioned.

Lasiurus ega males

Seasonal pattern (fig. 7). — The testes of adults in December and January contain a ma-

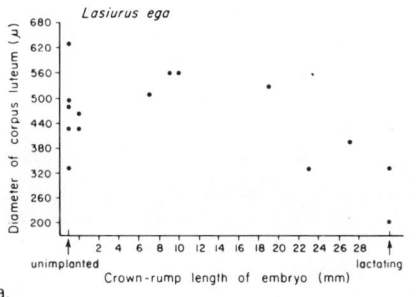
a.

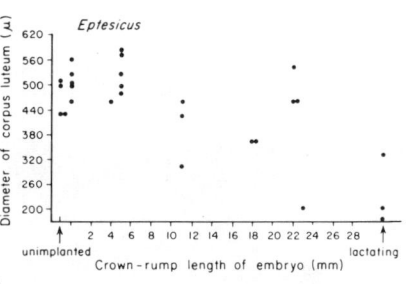
b.

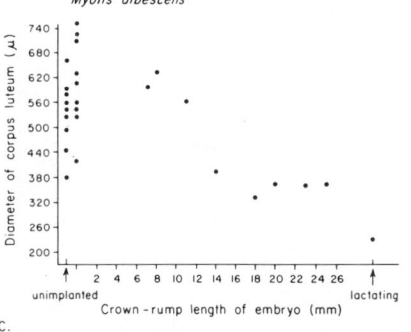
c.

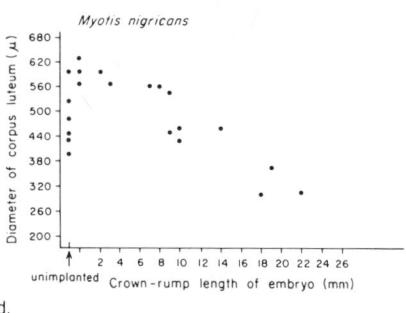
d.

Fig. 6. Change in diameter of the corpus luteum during pregnancy. a, *Lasiurus ega*; b, *Eptesicus furinalis*; c, *Myotis albescens*; d, *Myotis nigricans*.

jority of cells in early stages of spermatogenesis (plate 5). The average testis weight is about 7.5 mg. The tubules are crowded with meiotic cells and the lumina are small or closed. By March cells of all stages of spermatogenesis are found in the testes, and some individuals have spermatozoa in their epididymides. In April the testes reach their maximum weight of approximately 25 mg. The tubule lumina are large and the epididymides are swollen with spermatozoa. In May, June, and July (plate 5) the number of meiotic cells decreases, until by August almost none is present. By this time the lumina are small and only spermatogonia and Sertoli cells remain in the tubules. The epididymides contain spermatozoa at least until October, at which time the number of meioses in the testis tubules begins to increase in preparation for the next breeding season.

Young. – Four young male *Lasiurus*, 1 to 1½ months old, had small testes (6.6 to 13.4 mg). The lumina of the seminiferous tubules were small or closed, the tubules contained many cells in meiosis, and the epididymides were empty. In two cases spermatids were present. The testes resembled adult testes from the same period; young males are believed to be capable of breeding in their first year.

Interstitial tissue and accessory glands. – Seasonal changes occur in the interstitial cells of the testes of male *Lasiurus*. In the fall (March-May), when spermatogenesis occurs, the diameters of the nuclei of the interstitial cells are greatest, the nuclei are rounded, and the cells are large (plate 5). At other times the cells and nuclei are smaller, and the nuclei appear to be shriveled. The size of the accessory glands (in this case, measured as the distance from the base of the bladder to the cephalic end of the prostate; fig. 8a) follows a similar pattern (fig. 9a). The interstitial cells appear to be most active in March, April, and early May, while the size of the accessory glands remains large until July or August (plate 5). Males in July in particular had enlarged, swollen accessory glands, while their interstitial cells were small and had small, shriveled nuclei.

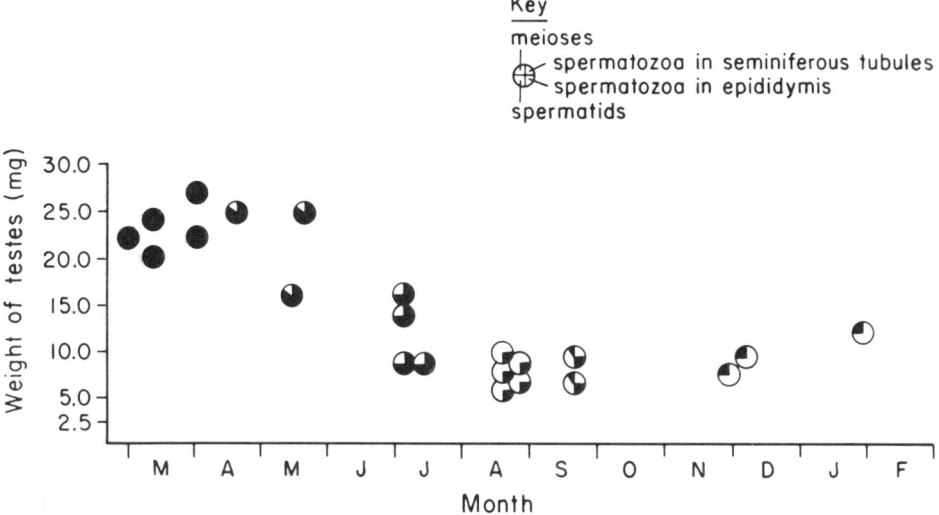

Fig. 7. Annual testicular cycle of male *Lasiurus ega*. Only males whose testes were examined microscopically are represented. Each symbol represents one individual. The circles are subdivided into quadrants, each representing one phase of spermatogenesis (see key). Shading in a quadrant representing a given stage indicates that cells in that stage are present, with partial shading indicating less than full activity.

a. *Lasiurus ega* ♂ accessory glands

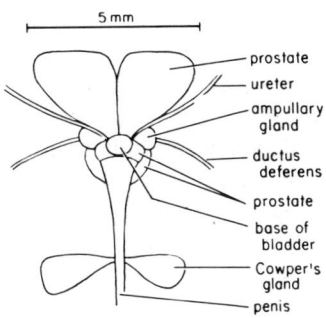

b. *Eptesicus* ♂ accessory glands

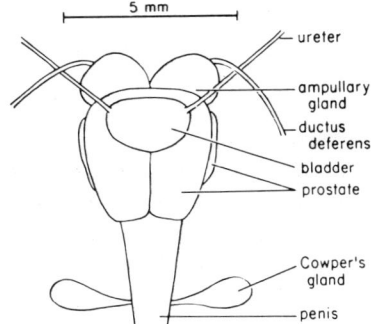

c. *Myotis albescens* ♂ accessory glands

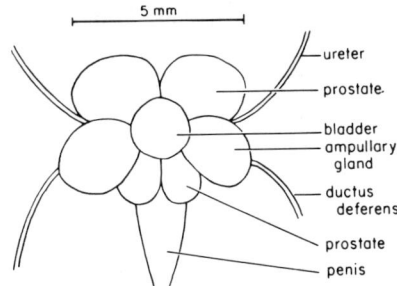

d. *Myotis nigricans* ♂ accessory glands

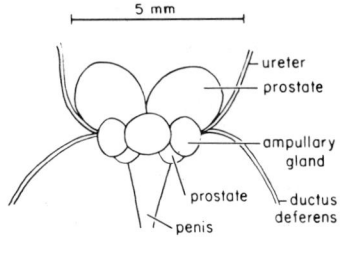

Fig. 8. Male accessory reproductive glands. a, *Lasiurus ega*; b, *Eptesicus furinalis*; c, *Myotis albescens*; d, *Myotis nigricans*.

a. *Lasiurus ega*

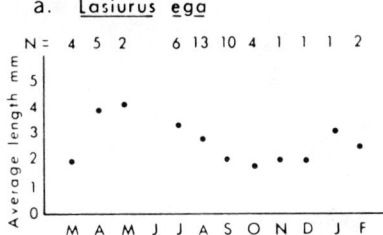

b. *Eptesicus* sp.

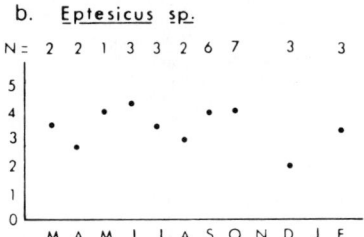

c. *Myotis albescens*

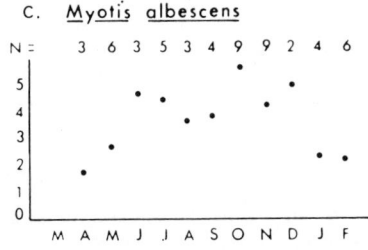

d. *Myotis nigricans*

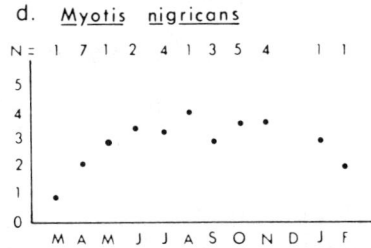

Fig. 9. Seasonal changes in mean length of the male accessory reproductive glands. a, *Lasiurus ega*; b, *Eptesicus furinalis*; c, *Myotis albescens*; d, *Myotis nigricans*.

Eptesicus furinalis females

Seasonal pattern (fig. 10). — Females with spermatozoa in their uteri are first found in May. Pregnancies first appear in late July and August, and the duration of pregnancy is slightly more than 3 months. No difference in timing is detectable between individuals from the Eastern Region and from the Chaco. The presence of spermatozoa in the uteri of females that have recently given birth indicates that copulation quickly follows parturition. There is little, if any, delay between this post-partum copulation and ovulation, and all females observed were simultaneously pregnant and lactating in December. Parturition for the second breeding period is in January, suggesting that the gestation period for the second pregnancy may be shorter than the first. This would not be surprising; Pearson *et al.*, (1952), Racey (1973), and others suggest that cold temperatures prolong gestation, and temperatures in August and September are much lower than in November and December. Unfortunately, too few records were obtained for the summer breeding period to adequately document this phenomenon for Paraguayan bats. Because few bats were captured in December and January, the evidence for a second breeding period consists primarily of the occurrence of very early pregnancies in December and of lactation in January.

The average number of embryos (for females in which the crown-rump length of the embryos is greater than 10 mm, see below) for the first breeding period is 1.9; the mode, 2; the range, 1-2. The number of embryos in females taken during the second breeding period is invariably one (table 3).

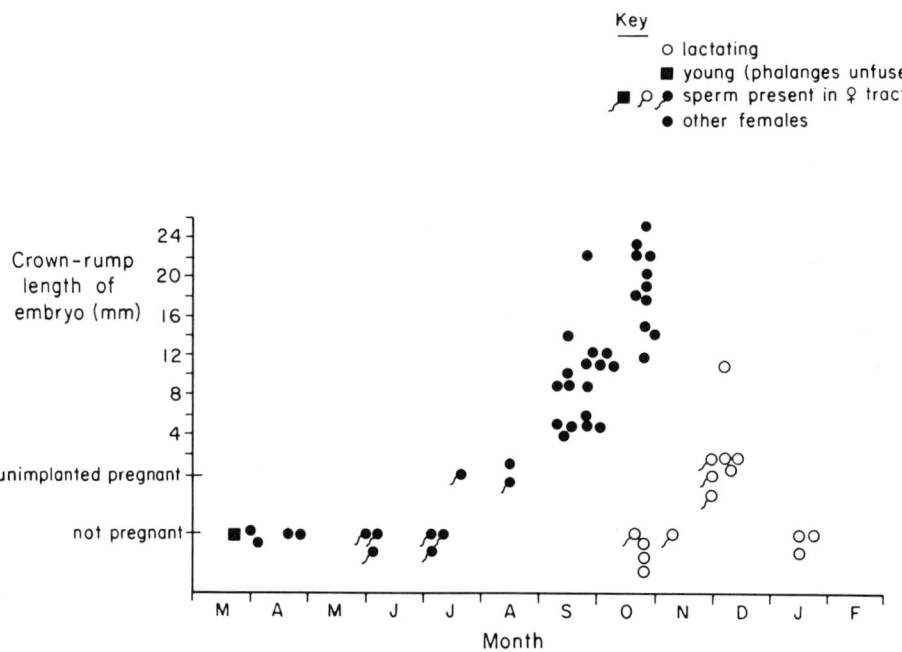

Fig. 10. Annual breeding pattern of female *Eptesicus furinalis*. Only females whose ovaries were examined microscopically, or which were pregnant, are represented.

TABLE 3

Relationship of Number of Corpora Lutea, Number of Embryos, and Embryo Size in *Eptesicus furinalis*

	First breeding period				Second breeding period		
Bat no.	No. CL	No. embryos	Size embryos	Bat no.	No. CL	No. embryos	Size embryos
1	4	4	tubal ova	1	1	1	morula
2	3	3	morula	2	1	1	morula
3	3	2-3	early placenta	3	1	1	morula
4	5	4	CR=3mm	4	1	1	early placenta
5	3	3	CR=4	5	1	1	early placenta
6	3	3	4	6	1	1	early placenta
7	5	4	4	7	1	1	early placenta
8	3	2	5	8	1	1	CR=11
9	3	2	5				
10	3	2	11				
11	4	2	11				
12	4	2	18				
13	3	1	22				
14	3	2	22				
15	4	2	22				
16	3	2	23				

Anatomy (table 2). — The uterine horns of nonpregnant females are approximately equal, with dimensions of 2 mm X 0.7 mm. The ovaries are round to oval in cross section, approximately 1.3 mm in diameter, and without lobes or fissures. Neither follicles nor corpora lutea are visible to the naked eye. A rete ovarii is usually present but smaller than that of female *Lasiurus ega*. There are also fewer medullary cords, and they do not form an important part of the medulla (plate 6). The ovaries are larger than those of *Lasiurus* and contain more interstitial tissue and fewer follicles.

Follicles. — Ovaries from females in fall (April and May) contain several follicles with diameters from 100 to 250 μ, but those to be ovulated are not recognizable. The single female captured in June contained at least 15 follicles with diameters greater than 230 μ, and a few as large as 260 μ. By early July, three to five follicles per female have enlarged to about 300 μ and presumably are those which will be ovulated in late July or early August. Early in the pregnancy that follows all remaining large follicles disappear from the ovaries. Toward the end of the first pregnancy (crown-rump, CR, length of the embryo equal to 22 to 23 mm) the size increases again, but in my samples the diameters never exceeded 230 μ. A single biovular follicle was found in each of two females.

Corpora lutea (fig. 6b, plate 6). — One female with tubal ova (in the 2 to 4 cell stage) had corpora lutea with large lumina containing a few free cells. They were not yet vascular, the borders were surrounded by the remnants of the theca externa, and paraluteal cells were probably present. The luteal cells had swollen nuclei with faint but distinct nucleoli. Other pre-implantation individuals had similar corpora, but most lacked a lumen and were moderately vascular. In some, the remains of the theca externa had already disappeared.

At implantation, vascularity is maximum. However, the change in vascularity over the life of the corpus luteum is very slight compared with the change in *Myotis* (see below). The most marked changes are in the nuclei and in the nature of the border of the corpus luteum. By the time a crown-rump length of 18 mm is achieved, the nuclei are shriveled and the nucleoli are very faint (plate 6). The border of the corpus is less distinct, appearing to merge with the stroma. By late pregnancy (CR = 23 mm), the corpus luteum is still recognizable, but it is very difficult to distinguish from the stroma.

Many lactating individuals have recognizable corpora, suggesting that the corpus luteum persists longer in females of this species than in female *Myotis*. The remnants are usually seen as a light area in the ovarian stroma, where the density of nuclei is lower than elsewhere.

Two peculiarities of breeding *Eptesicus* were noted. First, pregnant females from the first breeding period almost always have more corpora lutea than embryos. The difference between the number of embryos and the number of corpora lutea increases as the embryos increase in size (table 3), so that a significant negative correlation exists between size of embryos and number of embryos (Spearmann Rank Correlation Coefficient r = -.85, p < .01). Apparently more embryos are produced than can be successfully brought to term, and the number is reduced during gestation, presumably by resorption. This phenomenon occurs also in north temperate populations of *Eptesicus fuscus* (Wimsatt, 1945). Second, the number of embryos in the second breeding period is invariably one, and there is always only one corpus luteum (table 3).

Eptesicus furinalis males

Seasonal pattern (fig. 11, plate 7). — The available data suggest that male *Eptesicus* have two peaks of testicular activity. Testes from bats captured during the summer months are small and contain many meiotic configurations. During the fall spermatogenesis accelerates, and mature spermatozoa are first found in the epididymides in late April. From April through early June testis weight is maximum. Then, beginning in mid-June testicular activity declines. Two males from this month had large testes, and epididymides swollen with spermatozoa, but their seminiferous tubules lacked meiotic configurations and the lumina were large, as if the contents had been spent. Unfortunately, only two adult males were captured during July and August. The first, in July, had small testes, no cells in meiosis, few spermatozoa or spermatids in the seminiferous tubules, but epididymides swollen with spermatozoa. The second, in August, had empty epididymides but abundant meiotic configurations in the testis tubules. By early September testis size has increased and spermatids and spermatozoa are abundant in the testes, though the epididymides are not swollen until late September. Tes-

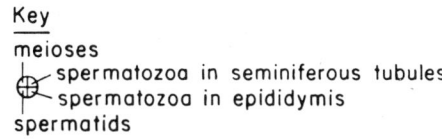
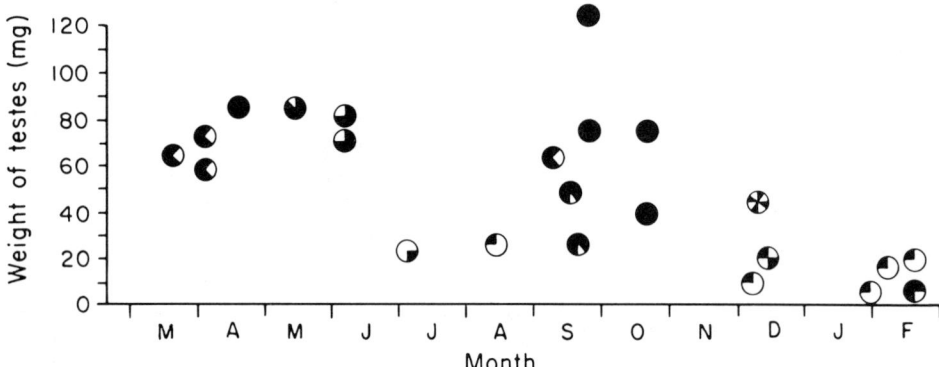

Fig. 11. Annual testicular cycle of male *Eptesicus furinalis*. Only males whose testes were examined microscopically are represented. See explanation of figure 7.

tis size and activity begin to decline in December, and are probably minimal in January.

Young. — The testes of two young male *Eptesicus* were sectioned. One, born in October-November and captured in early December, had testes weighing only 5.8 mg and small seminiferous tubules without lumina that contained only spermatogonia and Sertoli cells. The epididymal tubules were also small and empty. The second young male was caught in mid-February and was probably also born in October or November. The testis tubules, which contained a moderate number of meiotic configurations but no spermatids or spermatogonia, were of medium size but lacked a lumen. The epididymal tubules were small and empty. Testes of adult males caught during February were similar, but contained more cells in meiosis.

Interstitial tissue and accessory glands. — Young male *Eptesicus* are remarkable for the large number of interstitial cells in their testes. The cells and nuclei are smaller and the nuclei more involuted than those of older males. Rather than occurring in discrete clumps as in older animals, the cells form a continuous matrix about the tubules. The testes of a young male caught in December (age 1-2 months) were estimated to be 35% interstitial tissue by volume; the testes of a slightly older male, caught in February, were about 25% interstitial tissue. Adult testes are, on the average, composed of 5% interstitial tissue by volume. Much of the decrease in relative prominence of interstitial tissue in adults can be accounted for by the increase in volume of the testis, rather than by any decrease in the volume of interstitial tissue with age.

Seasonal changes occur in the interstitial tissue and accessory glands, but they are not as marked as the changes in male *Lasiurus* (plates 5, 7). Interstitial cells and their nuclei are largest during the periods of copulation, March to June and September to October. The accessory glands (fig. 9b) are enlarged at the same time the interstitial cells appear to be most active. Thus male *Eptesicus* differ from male *Lasiurus*, in which the accessory glands remain large after the interstitial tissue involutes.

20 *University of California Publications in Zoology*

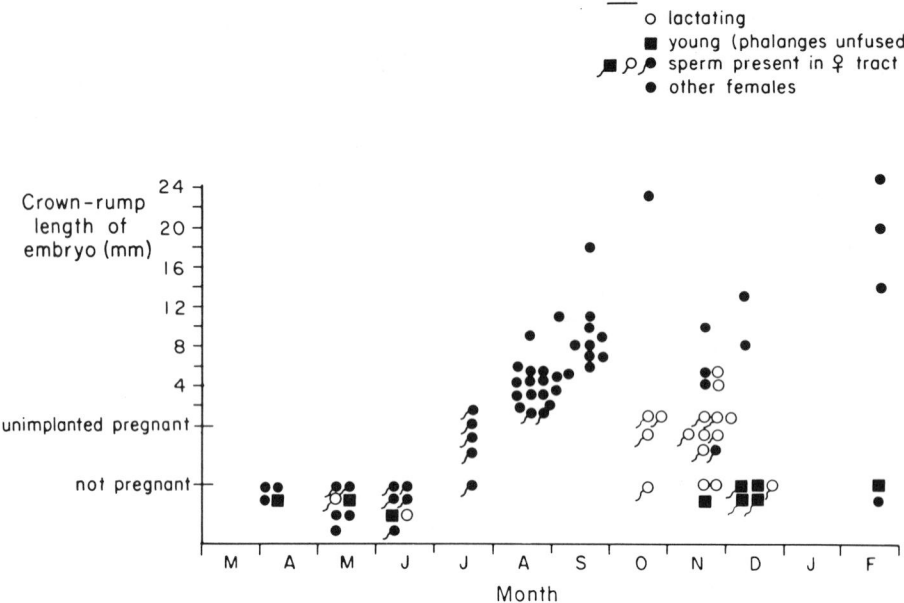

Fig. 12. Annual breeding pattern of female *Myotis albescens*. Only females whose ovaries were examined microscopically, or which were pregnant, are represented.

Male *Eptesicus* differ from males of the other three species examined in that the accessory reproductive gland projecting furthest cephalad is a lobe of the ampullary gland rather than of the prostate (fig. 8b).

Myotis albescens females

Seasonal pattern (fig. 12). — The appearance in May of spermatozoa in the female reproductive tracts marks the beginning of the breeding season, nearly 2 months prior to the first ovulations in July. Parturition takes place in October, followed by copulation and a second pregnancy. Considerable scatter occurs, however, in the data concerning the second pregnancy, and there is a possibility that some females breed a third time in January, February, and March. Unfortunately I was unable to obtain *Myotis* from mid-December through late February. Lactation in May and June (fig. 12) is consistent with either a third breeding period, a delay in the second breeding period by some individuals, or the late breeding of young females. By early April, the breeding season is over. Ten females were collected in early April, 10 in mid-May, and 10 in mid-June; none of these was pregnant.

The gestation period is three months or slightly less. Lactation continues for about one month. The gestation period for the second and third pregnancies may be shorter than for the first. Unfortunately, the size and timing of the samples precludes a precise determination of gestation periods (see *Eptesicus*, females, above). Female *Myotis albescens* are invariably monotocous.

Anatomy (table 2). — The uterine cornua of nulliparous females are approximately equal in size. In parous females the right horn is larger than the left. The horns of parous females examined shortly before they become pregnant in July had an average length of 1.8 mm (right side) and 1.3 mm (left side), and widths of 1.0 mm (both sides). Implantation always occurs on the right side; the ovary providing the ovum was not identified. The ovaries are round to oval in cross section and about 1 mm in diameter.

The ovaries of *M. albescens* usually have fewer medullary cords than those of *Lasiurus*. A rete is present and of medium to large size. The ovaries of *M. albescens* are larger than those of *M. nigricans*, and have proportionately more space occupied by interstitial tissue and less by follicles.

Follicles. — At the time copulation begins there are four or five follicles about 250 μ in diameter (plate 8). The diameter increases slightly in June (to 265 μ), but the ovum which will be ovulated is not yet recognizable. Only one nonpregnant female was captured in late July. She had one very large follicle (430 μ), and four or five follicles of about 250 μ diameter. Since the largest follicle appeared to be atretic, and all other females had ovulated by this time, this individual may have been abnormal. The number and average size of follicles increases again in late pregnancy. In November most females examined (both lactating and simultaneously lactating and pregnant) had a few follicles exceeding 300 μ in diameter. All females from late February (both nonpregnant and late pregnant) had ovaries with moderate numbers of small and medium follicles (less than 240 μ). No polyovular follicles were found.

Corpora lutea (fig. 6c). — The youngest corpus luteum seen was in a female with an 8-cell morula in her uterus. The corpus luteum had a diameter of 380 μ, no lumen, and was already moderately to extensively vascular with most vessels capillaries. The nuclei of the luteal cells were spherical and contained moderately distinct nucleoli. Surrounding the corpus luteum was a very narrow, irregular zone of paraluteal cells. Outside the paraluteal zone the theca externa of the ovulated follicle was still recognizable. The corpus of this individual was fairly typical of other preimplantation females (plate 8). Such corpora range in diameter from 380 μ to 660 μ, and a small lumen is sometimes present.

By the time the placenta has formed, several changes take place in the corpus luteum. The nuclei of the luteal cells become more swollen and the nucleoli very prominent. Vascularization increases and larger vessels are present. When the embryo reaches a crown-rump length of about 10 mm, the diameter decreases (fig. 6c); the nuclei of the luteal cells begin to shrivel and the nucleoli decrease in prominence. By this time the vascularity of the corpus has decreased and proportionately fewer capillaries and more large vessels are present (plate 8). These changes suggest a more rapid decrease in luteal function during mid-pregnancy than is true of either *Eptesicus furinalis* or *Lasiurus ega* in Paraguay. By late pregnancy the corpus luteum is small and indistinct, the nuclei are shriveled and the nucleoli have almost disappeared. The gross morphologic difference between luteal cells and interstitial cells has diminished, making the border of the corpus hard to distinguish under low magnification. Corpora lutea were present in only two of fourteen lactating females, suggesting that the corpus disappears soon after parturition.

Young. — The ovaries from a very young female contained only small and medium-sized follicles (less than 120 μ in diameter), with few atretic follicles. The number of medium to large follicles increases with age, as does the number of atretic follicles. Some young born in October or November had one to two large (greater than 300 μ) follicles by mid-December. These females had sperm in their uteri, suggesting that the large follicles might soon be ovulated. The follicles of one young female taken in February and one taken in June were smaller than 250 μ in diameter, though these individuals were apparently older (as indicated by bone development) than those taken in December.

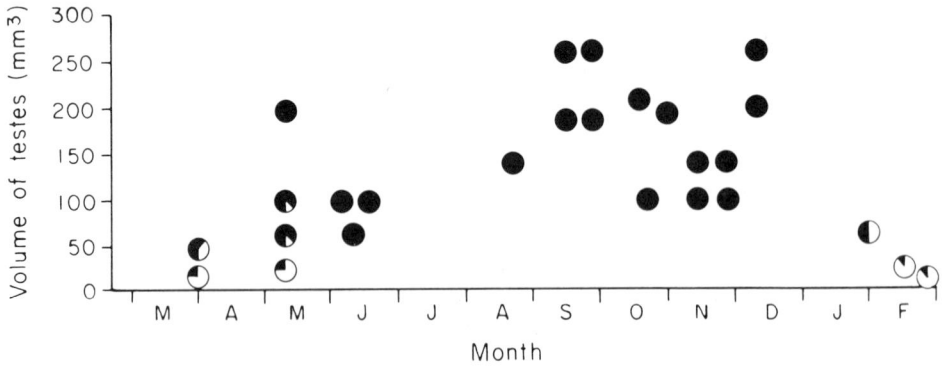

Fig. 13. Annual testicular cycle of male *Myotis albescens*. Only males whose testes were examined microscopically are represented. See explanation of figure 7.

Myotis albescens males

Seasonal pattern (fig. 13). — Testes of adults are smallest during the late summer (January-March), when their volume ranges from 50 to 75 mm^3. At this time testis tubules are of small to medium size and contain few meiotic configurations and no spermatids or spermatozoa (plate 9). By April the number of cells undergoing meiosis has increased, fully formed spermatozoa are present in the testis tubules and, in a few individuals, in the epididymides as well. Testis size, however, does not reach a maximum until spring (September), when some testes have volumes greater than 250 mm^3. At this time, the testis tubules are large and the lumina are of medium size. Testes remain large and active at least into December (plate 9, fig. 13).

Young. — Testes of young males captured in January, February, April, and June were sectioned. In those collected in January and February, and in one collected in June, there were few cells in meiosis and no spermatids or spermatozoa. Young males collected in April, and one young male from June, had testes with abundant meiotic configurations, while adult males taken at these times also contained spermatids and sometimes spermatozoa. Inferences concerning the precise age of the young *Myotis* are difficult both because of the imprecision of the aging technique, and because of the wide scatter in times of birth. Thus the age at which males of this species first breed remains in doubt, but is probably less than one year.

Interstitial tissue and accessory glands. — Seasonal changes in interstitial tissue and accessory glands occur, but are difficult to measure (plate 9). The diameters of interstitial cell nuclei change minimally. The cells and nuclei are most swollen from May through December, and most involuted in January and February. The accessory glands (in this case, the prostate; fig. 8c) are also largest from May until December (fig. 9c).

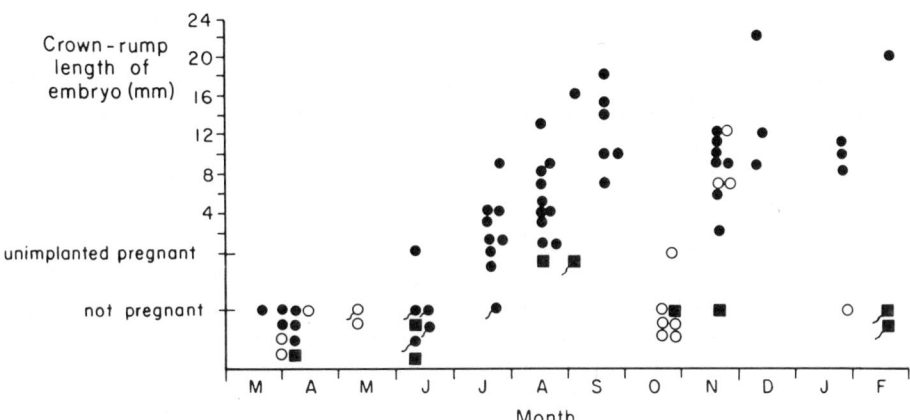

Fig. 14. Annual breeding pattern of female *Myotis nigricans*. Only females whose ovaries were examined microscopically, or which were pregnant, are represented.

Myotis nigricans females

Seasonal pattern (fig. 14). – The seasonal pattern of breeding by female *M. nigricans* resembles that of *M. albescens*, but is not as well defined. Females showing some indication of breeding (presence of sperm in the uterus, pregnancy, or lactation) were found in every month, despite small sample sizes. April and May appear to be the months of least reproductive activity. For most of the population, copulation probably occurs in May and continues in June. Some pregnancies were recorded in June (1 of 7 females) and July (8 of 9 females). By late August and in September all females are pregnant, and most have well-developed fetuses. Parturition takes place by late October. In contrast to *M. albescens* and *Eptesicus*, copulation for the second breeding period is delayed. None of the lactating females caught in October had spermatozoa in her uterus. However, two females in mid-pregnancy were lactating, one in November and one in December, so copulation and ovulation can occur before lactation ends.

If fetal development occurs at the same rate in all breeding periods, then most parturitions for the second period take place in late December and early January. The presence of pregnant females in late February indicates either a third breeding period for some individuals, considerably more scatter in the second breeding period than in the first, or perhaps the first breeding of individuals born in October.

Myotis nigricans females are monotocous. The gestation period is 3 months or slightly less, and lactation lasts for about a month.

Anatomy (table 2). – The reproductive tracts of *Myotis nigricans* resemble those of *M. albescens*. The uterine horns of nulliparous females are equal, while those of parous females are not. Typical uterine dimensions for a parous female are 1.9 mm length X 1.1 mm diameter for the right horn, and 1.5 mm X 1.0 mm for the left horn. The ovaries are 0.7-0.8 mm in diameter. Implantation always takes place on the right side, but it was not determined which ovary provides the ovum.

The ovaries contain less interstitial tissue relative to their volume than do those of *M. albescens* (plate 10). The rete are medium to large, but the epoöphoron tubules are usually small.

Follicles. – Among nonpregnant adults there appears to be no consistent seasonal pattern of folliculogenesis. In about one-third of the individuals examined, one ovary is larger than the other, or contains the majority of large follicles. In general, nonpregnant females have moderate to large numbers of follicles of all sizes, and there are usually at least 8-10 follicles with a diameter of 230 μ or more (plate 10).

Corpus luteum. – Preimplantation ovaries have corpora lutea ranging from 400 μ to 600 μ in diameter, some with a small lumen (fig. 6d; plate 10). The corpora are usually moderately vascular, with relatively more capillaries than later in pregnancy. Remnants of the theca externa are usually recognizable, and some paraluteal cells are present. The nuclei of most luteal cells are swollen and contain moderately prominent nucleoli. The corpora lutea of females with recently implanted embryos are similar, but vessels of all sizes, especially capillaries, are abundant. The nuclei of the luteal cells are swollen and contain prominent nucleoli (plate 10). The theca externa has disappeared, and the border of the corpus is indistinct. A few cells resembling paraluteal cells are present. By the time the crown-rump length of the embryo reaches 10 mm, the level of vascularity has decreased noticeably, and the prominence of large vessels relative to capillaries has increased. Masses of small cells with small, dark, irregularly shaped nuclei abound around the periphery of the corpus luteum, and paraluteal cells have disappeared. The nuclei and nucleoli of most luteal cells remain swollen and very prominent. By the time the embryo is 18 mm long, the nuclei are shriveled and nucleoli are present but not prominent (plate 10). Vascularity is reduced and the border of the corpus luteum is indistinct. At the 23 mm stage, shortly before birth, the nuclei are shriveled, the nucleoli have almost disappeared, and there is almost no vascularization. In an ovary belonging to an animal considered recently post-partum, no obvious corpus luteum was found in the sections. Old corpora lutea were never found in lactating females.

In summary, vascularity of the new corpus luteum increases swiftly, reaches a maximum around the time of implantation, and gradually subsides. The prominence of the nucleoli and the swelling of the nuclei change similarly. As in *M. albescens*, the diameter of the corpus and the prominence of the nucleoli decrease abruptly around 12 mm crown-rump length (fig. 6c, d).

Young. – Ovaries from five nonpregnant juvenile females were sectioned. The four youngest had numerous polyovular follicles, a condition never found in adults of this species (plate 10). These follicles were usually atretic. The older juveniles had numerous follicles of all sizes, including at least ten follicles per individual with a diameter greater than 250 μ.

Myotis nigricans males

Seasonal pattern (fig. 15). – There is no discernible seasonal pattern of spermatogenesis or testis volume among adult males: all have spermatozoa in their seminiferous tubules and in their epididymides at all times of the year (plate 11). At no time, however, are the epididymides as swollen or packed with spermatozoa as they are in the other three species (plate 3b).

Male *Myotis nigricans* are notable for the small size of their testes relative to body weight. The average testis volume of males in breeding condition (body weight 3-5 gm) is about 10 mm³. In contrast, male *Myotis albescens* in breeding condition (body weight 5-6 gm) have testes approximately 200 mm³ in volume (figs. 13, 15; plate 3b).

Young. — Only the youngest individuals lacked spermatozoa in their epididymides. Most young males examined had more meiotic configurations than adults and would probably soon be capable of breeding. One young male differed from adults only in having fewer spermatids and spermatozoa and more cells in meiosis. Mature spermatozoa were present in the seminiferous tubules and epididymides. It therefore is likely that male *M. nigricans* breed well before the end of their first year.

Interstitial tissue and accessory glands. — No seasonal change was detected in the interstitial tissue (plate 11), but the accessory reproductive glands (fig. 8d) are slightly smaller from December through April than during the rest of the year (fig. 9d). Some breeding occurs during this interval, however, indicating that the apparent decrease in size may be unimportant or due to sampling error.

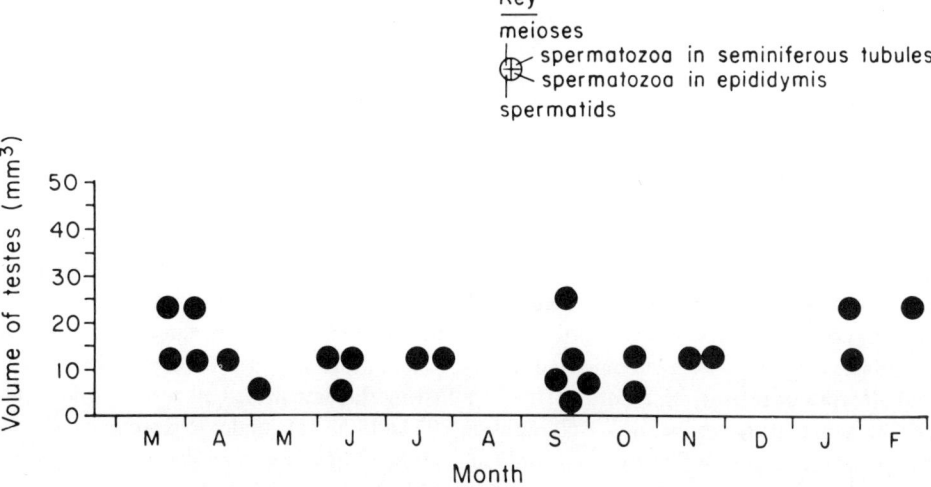

Fig. 15. Annual testicular cycle of male *Myotis nigricans*. Only males whose testes were examined microscopically are represented. See explanation of figure 7.

TEMPERATURE AND ACTIVITY

Several types of evidence suggest that Paraguayan vespertilionids do not hibernate. First, weather patterns make hibernation improbable. Minimum temperatures rarely remain below 10°C for more than a few days at a time, and the coldest nights are usually accompanied by warm, clear days. Cold periods alternate with warm periods when the daytime temperature may exceed 30°C. The average daily maximum temperature for the coldest month at Pozo Colorado is 25°C (fig. 3), too warm to permit hibernation by bats unable to retreat to hibernacula. Second, no annual pattern of fat storage resembling that of temperate hibernators was seen. Third, vespertilionids were caught in nets (*i.e.*, while flying) every month of the year, and on the coldest nights that I recorded. Above 7° to 8°C little, if any, reduction of activity was observed, though this was very difficult to measure.

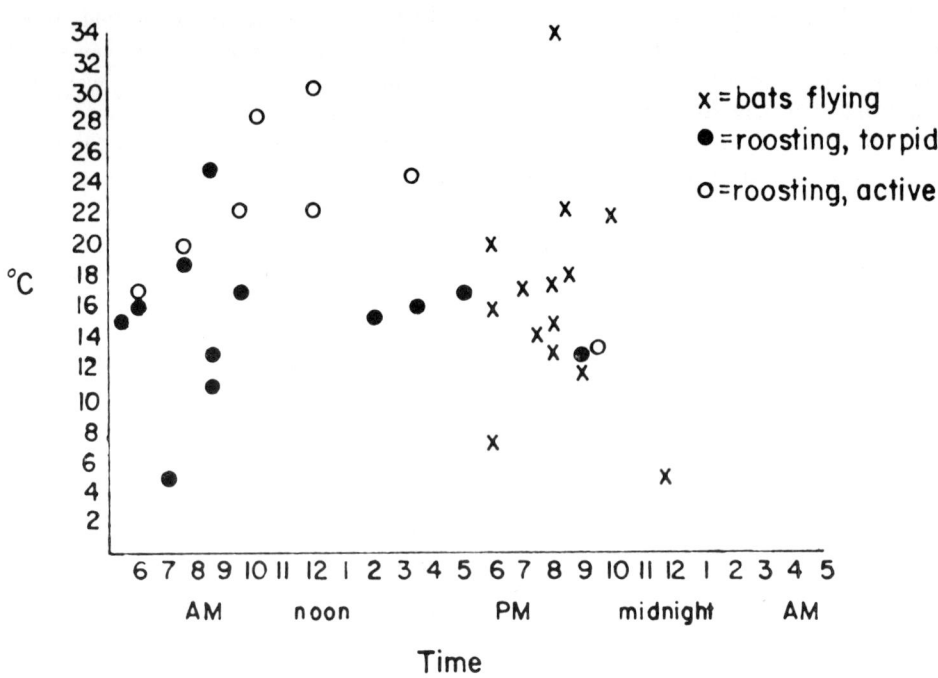

Fig. 16. Activity of bats (all species) as a function of time and temperature.

These arguments make the occurrence of lengthy hibernation unlikely. Daily torpor occurs, however, and is probably the state in which bats pass most of the days during the cold season. Data concerning daily torpor were gathered during daytime searches for bats in palm log roofs. When bats were encountered, the air temperature was measured, and the bats' state (torpid or active) was recorded (fig. 16). During the day, most bats were torpid when the air temperature was below 20°C. Between 20° and 25° bats under logs were usually active; only one group of five groups examined at these temperatures was torpid. At higher temperatures bats were always active and flew off immediately when the log was raised. Thus diurnal torpor is possible from approximately 25° to 5°C (the lowest temperature at which observations were made).

There is some evidence that social grouping affects torpor. At 15° to 17° the members of one large group of *Myotis* were active, while solitary individuals from the same roof at the same time were torpid.

An important feature of Chaco habitat for bats is the lack of suitable hibernacula. There are no caves. The most appropriate sites for roosts are houses, still a rare resource for bats. Because spaces are usually left between the roof and wall for ventilation, and because roofs are usually thin and uninsulated, temperatures in houses must fluctuate considerably even in the most protected nooks and crannies. Furthermore, most *Myotis* at Rincón Charrua left the more protected indoor roost and moved to palm log roofs during the winter. Temperatures under the logs were within 2°C of the air temperature (in the shade) when the logs were shaded, and were probably higher than the air temperature when logs were in the sun. Bats may use the logs in the winter because they warm faster in the morning, and they may use thick-walled buildings in the summer to avoid extreme heat. Unfortunately, I cannot be certain that the shift from the indoor roost to the palm log roosts seen at Rincón Charrua was due to climatic changes rather than to human disturbance of the bats.

I conclude that hibernation by bats in the Paraguayan Chaco is unlikely. Ambient temperatures are too high during much of the winter, no suitable hibernacula are available, fat is not stored, and bats were seen flying under most conditions. Even in the Región Oriental, hibernation by *Eptesicus* and *Lasiurus* is unlikely. Although caves are present in some areas, neither species was ever found to inhabit them. Their preferred roosts are at least as exposed to high temperatures and temperature fluctuations as *Myotis* roosts in the Chaco, and they too were observed flying under the coldest conditions I experienced.

AGGREGATIONS OF *MYOTIS NIGRICANS* AND *MYOTIS ALBESCENS*

On cool mornings, bats roosting in roofs made of split palm logs were torpid and were easily captured when I lifted the upper logs. In this manner I gathered information on aggregations of *Myotis nigricans* and *M. albescens* at Rincón Charrua from July through September, 1973. During this period females of both species advanced from early to late pregnancy.

The most common species found under the logs was *M. nigricans*, the sexes of which have different roosting habits (table 4). Males were usually found singly, while females tended to occur in groups. The percentage of solitary females varied from 25% (N = 40 in-

TABLE 4

Aggregations of *Myotis nigricans*

Males		Females	
x No. of bats under a log	f No. of logs with x bats	x	f
0	1400	0	1396
1	70	1	14
2	1	2	2
3	1	3	5
4	0	4	1
5	0	5	2
>5	0	>5	7

Three sampling periods, 28 July, 20 August, and 22 September are summed here.

These distributions differ significantly at the .01 level of confidence (Kolmogorov-Smirnov Two Sample Test).

dividuals) in late July, to 0% (N = 27 individuals) in late September. The remaining females occurred in all-female groups of two to ten individuals, or in groups containing one male and one to thirteen females. No consistent differences in reproductive condition were found between females roosting singly, in all-female groups, and in groups of several females with a single male.

The groups exhibited a remarkable degree of cohesiveness over the three month period. Marking studies showed that females were usually found associated with the same females from one sampling period to the next. When groups changed, they did so by breaking into sub-groups, or coalescing to form larger groups, rather than by random reassortment of individuals. Although as many as twenty-eight males of *M. nigricans* were handled per census, the same three individuals were always found with groups of females. Each of these occurred repeatedly with the same nucleus of females (though at times individuals might be missing from the group). This suggests the occurrence of harems.

While individuals of *Myotis albescens* also roost under palm logs, their pattern of assortment is very different from that of individuals of *M. nigricans*. Solitary individuals were occasionally found, but most bats lived in large groups. Two groups were recorded during the July-September sampling period: one consisting of twelve males and two females; the other, of ten males and three females. Two or three *M. nigricans* were also present in each group.

Bats of both species also roost inside buildings. From several hundred to over one thousand bats cluster together in roosts of this type, and no data on groupings within the cluster could be obtained. Both sexes of both species are found together, and lactating females with young are also present. I found no nursery colonies of the type described for north temperate vespertilionids.

DISCUSSION

Patterns of Breeding

Females of the four species of bats studied give birth in September or October. In the subsequent months the pattern of births differs from species to species (fig. 17): *Lasiurus* females do not breed again; *Eptesicus* females have a post-partum estrus and breed once more; and both species of *Myotis* breed either one or two more times before May. The timing of breeding thus results in few young being weaned during the winter (from May through September). The reproductive cycles of many populations of bats are thought to be timed so that young are weaned at the most favorable time of year (see Fleming *et al.*, 1972). The weather in Paraguay is cool from May through September. Although abundance of insects was not measured, there is little doubt that flying insects are less available to bats in winter because of a reduction in the number of insects and in the activity of those present (see Taylor, 1963). It is therefore likely that the hiatus in breeding during the southern winter is at least partly due to scarcity of food.

Another factor that may influence breeding in winter is the direct effect of temperature on the female bats. Low temperatures are known to retard gestation in several north temperate species (Pearson *et al.*, 1952; Orr, 1954; Dwyer, 1971; Racey, 1973; Tuttle, 1975). In Paraguay, gestation begins in July, August, or September, while temperatures are still low, suggesting that breeding patterns are not determined by the detrimental effect of cold on embryonic growth rates. However, an elucidation of the effect of temperature on the length of gestation would require data from several years and better weather records than are now available.

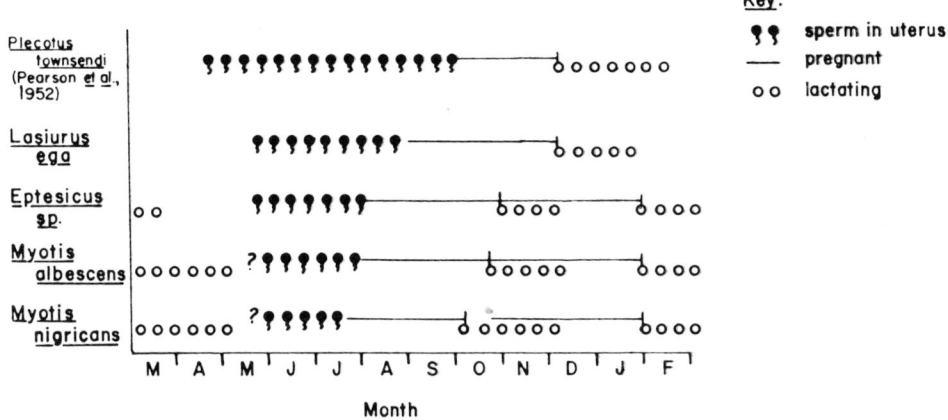

Fig. 17. Breeding patterns of female vespertilionid bats in Paraguay compared to that of *Plecotus townsendi* (after Pearson et al., 1952) in North America. The pattern of *Plecotus* has been advanced six months to compensate for the difference in seasons between northern and southern hemispheres.

Low temperatures may also directly affect the survival and growth of young bats (see Tuttle, 1975).

The reasons why one species should breed once, one twice, and the remaining two either two or three times, are not known. The differences could be due to reliance on different insects for food, but data are not available on food preferences. The evolutionary history of populations of each species, and their current relationship with populations in different but contiguous environments may also be important.

The timing of spermatogenesis also differs among the species (fig. 18). Male *Myotis nigricans* are able to breed continuously. No mature males lacked sperm in their epididymides, and no seasonal differences were detectable in the testes. For male *Myotis albescens*, the period of fertility is more limited. Spermatozoa are present in the epididymides from May through December and during this period spermatozoa appear in the uteri of most nonpregnant females. Male *Eptesicus* have a similar pattern, except during midwinter (July to August), when they neither produce nor store spermatozoa. The testes and epididymides of male *Eptesicus* are at a peak in May and in October, when spermatozoa are found in the uteri of the females. Male *Lasiurus* have the shortest breeding season. Spermatozoa are present in the males from May through September or October, and the uteri of females are crowded with spermatozoa from May until August.

The reasons for the interspecific differences among males are obscure. Males of all four species have spermatozoa available during early winter, when copulation occurs in at least three of the species (fig. 18). Spermatozoa are also available in males of the four species during late winter, when copulation may also occur. The time when spermatozoa are first and last matured differs among the species, and is not easily related to the female cycles. The critical time of year with respect to the production of spermatozoa may be when spermatogenesis does not (cannot?) take place. Spermatogenesis is continual for *Myotis nigricans*. Summing the other species, meiotic configurations can be found during all months of the year, but few or no spermatids are found from mid-December until mid-February, and no spermatozoa are present until early April. The cessation of spermatogene-

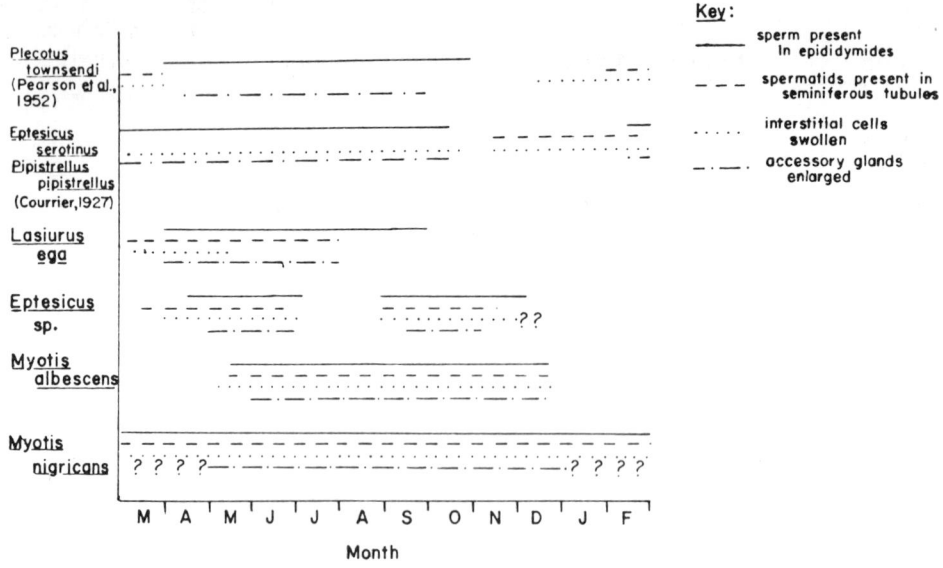

Fig. 18. Breeding patterns of male vespertilionid bats in Paraguay compared to several species of bats in North America and Europe. The patterns of *Plecotus townsendi* (after Pearson et al., 1952), *Eptesicus serotinus*, and *Pipistrellus pipistrellus* (after Courrier, 1927) have been advanced six months to compensate for the difference in seasons between northern and southern hemispheres.

sis during these mid-summer months may be due to the sensitivity of spermatogenesis to heat (Waites and Setchell, 1969). Daytime temperatures in the shade in Paraguay are frequently above 40°C, and sometimes rise to 45°C. Weeks may pass when the nocturnal temperature rarely or never drops below 35°C. Caves or other places of moderate microclimate are lacking or scarce in the Paraguayan Chaco. Because the heat is continuous, even thick-walled buildings become too warm to provide refuge. Neotropical *Myotis* under severe heat stress accept a temporary heat load and allow their body temperatures to rise (McNab, 1969). Thus continual high temperatures may be detrimental to spermatogenesis.

The hypothesis appears to be contradicted by the ability of *Myotis nigricans* to produce sperm continually. This may perhaps be explained by the small body size of this species. The average body weight of *M. nigricans* is 3.5-4 gm, while the next smallest bat studied, *M. albescens*, weighs about 5 gm. Body temperatures are expected to decrease as weight decreases (McNab, 1969). Due to their smaller size, individuals of *M. nigricans* have a higher ratio of surface area to volume, and therefore cool faster. In some species of mammals (bats have not been examined), once spermatozoa have progressed to the cauda epididymis they are less sensitive to high temperatures (Glover and Young, 1963). The lower body temperature and higher cooling rate may enable individuals of *M. nigricans* to take advantage of brief cool periods to produce spermatozoa. A comparison of the male tracts of the two species supports this hypothesis (plate 3b). During the breeding season, male *M. albescens* have large testes similar to north temperate species of *Myotis*. Male *M. nigricans* have unusually small testes (less than 10% of the volume of the testes of *M. albescens*), and the epididymides are longer and thinner than those of *M. albescens* (plate 3b). Both characteristics facilitate cooling.

What is the advantage of continual spermatogenesis if breeding is not continual? While the pattern of reproduction of *M. nigricans* resembles that of *M. albescens* in general, the presence of a female in early pregnancy in June, and of a recognizable juvenile (*i.e.*, less than 4 months old) in August, suggests a low level of breeding at all times of year for Paraguayan populations of *Myotis nigricans*. The plausibility of a continuing low level of breeding is enhanced by the segregation of *M. nigricans* individuals into harems with both sexes present. Unfortunately the data concerning aggregations were obtained for the winter months only.

Storage of Spermatozoa

The evidence suggests that female vespertilionid bats in Paraguay store spermatozoa. Males and females first copulate in May in three, or perhaps all four of the species. Yet females of *M. albescens* do not become pregnant until late July, and females of *Lasiurus* and *Eptesicus*, not until August. The reproductive pattern of female *M. nigricans* is less clear, but copulation begins in May or June, and fertilization takes place in June or July. Thus at least three of the species resemble north temperate bats in that females are found with spermatozoa in their uteri several months before the first embryos appear. An important difference between north temperate and Paraguayan populations of vespertilionids is that Paraguayan bats do not hibernate. North temperate bats are believed to copulate both prior to entering hibernation and during hibernation (Guthrie, 1933; Pearson *et al.*, 1952; Wimsatt, 1944). Guthrie (1933) argues that spermatozoa from early matings are rapidly lost when females arouse from hibernation during winter, and that the function of winter copulations is to replace the lost spermatozoa. The uteri from mature females of *M. albescens, Lasiurus,* and *Eptesicus* captured in June, July and August contained spermatozoa. If spermatozoa are quickly lost by active females, then copulations must be frequent throughout the winter. The selective advantage of this system is not clear, though it could be a vestigial pattern of neither positive nor strongly negative value, a reflection of either temperate zone ancestry or genetic continuity with contemporary temperate zone populations.

Storage of spermatozoa by females would be no less puzzling than repeated copulations. Spermatozoa are present in the epididymides of the males until after conception by females. Indeed, spermatozoa are stored by males of *Lasiurus* for at least two months after regression of the testes. Thus, the earlier matings seem unnecessary. However, north temperate male vespertilionids also possess spermatozoa until after the females have conceived. Pearson *et al.*, (1952) found seemingly healthy spermatozoa in the epididymides of male *Plecotus townsendi* caught in May and June in California, while most females ovulate in March. An extended period of copulation may serve as insurance that all females are inseminated, or it may have evolved because males that copulate earlier are able to copulate with (and fertilize) more females.

Hibernation is currently thought to be a *sine qua non* of storage of spermatozoa (Wimsatt, 1960; McNab, 1974). This conclusion stems from the observation by Wimsatt (1944) and Guthrie (1933) that spermatozoa disappear from the female tracts when the bats are active, and on Rice's observation (1957) that populations of *Myotis austroriparius* that do not hibernate do not store spermatozoa, while those that do hibernate, do store spermatozoa. Storage of spermatozoa by nonhibernating neotropical bats would require a revision of this hypothesis.

My data neither confirm nor deny the storage of spermatozoa by female vespertilionids in Paraguay, but copulations are shown to occur well in advance of ovulation. To properly document the occurrence of storage of spermatozoa, it would be necessary to maintain female bats in isolation from May until August or September. Whether they store spermatozoa or not, the selective advantage of the pattern remains obscure.

Interstitial Tissue

The relationships among interstitial tissue, male accessory reproductive glands, and testes in bats have been much discussed because of the asynchrony that sometimes occurs between spermatogenesis, enlargement of the accessory glands, and copulation. In *Pipistrellus pipistrellus* and *Eptesicus serotinus* in the Old World, Courrier (1927) found that the interstitial tissue becomes active in the summer when the testes are growing (fig. 18), and remains active through the winter, though the testes involute in the fall. The accessory glands enlarge in late summer and remain large through the winter. These observations have been confirmed and expanded by Racey and Tam (1974), who found little or no morphological change in the interstitial tissue of *P. pipistrellus* during the yearly cycle, and continued dependence of the male accessory glands on testicular androgens. Pearson *et al.* (1952) found a similar relationship between testes and accessories in *Plecotus townsendi* up to a point; *viz.*, the accessory glands continue to grow after the testes begin to involute, and interstitial tissue is most abundant and the cells are largest during the summer. However, during the fall the interstitial tissue involutes while the accessory glands are still growing. Thus when the cells appear to be most active, the accessory glands are small, and after they have involuted, the glands reach their largest size and copulations occur. Krutzsch (1956), working with *Pipistrellus hesperus* in North America, also found continuing accessory gland growth after the involution of the interstitial tissue, as did Miller (1939) with *Myotis lucifugus* and *M. grisescens*.

Wimsatt (1960) hypothesized that hibernation retards the involution of the accessory glands when their supply of male hormone is withdrawn by the involution of the interstitial tissue. He further suggested that hormone may be stored in the testes or elsewhere in the body and released slowly during the winter. The relationship among the interstitial tissue, spermatogenesis, and the accessory glands in a population of non-hibernating bats which apparently store spermatozoa would be of particular interest with respect to this problem.

Unfortunately, the analysis of male patterns relative to these questions is beset by several problems. The first is the small size of some samples, especially during the critical fall and early winter months. The second concerns the measurement of the accessory glands. While the volume of the glands may change considerably during the year, the linear measurements change slightly. This is in contrast to most rodents, for example, in which the length of the seminal vesicle increases many times before breeding. Third, interstitial tissue activity is assumed to be correlated with the morphology of the interstitial cells, yet swollen cells and nuclei may not necessarily imply secretion of androgen (Pearson *et al.*, 1952; Racey and Tam, 1974). In spite of these problems, some conclusions are possible. In *Myotis nigricans*, *M. albescens,* and *Eptesicus furinalis*, the accessory glands are large only when the interstitial tissue appears to be active (fig. 18). However, the accessory glands of *Lasiurus ega* remain large for 1½ to 2 months after the interstitial tissue appears to involute. In this respect, *L. ega* resembles North American vespertilionids, except that *L. ega* do not hibernate. Further work, especially using a more direct assay of male hormones (such as used by Racey and Tam, 1974), is needed.

Post Partum Estrus

Female *Eptesicus* and *Myotis albescens* mate soon after parturition. That a post partum estrus occurs is indicated by the presence of spermatozoa in recently parturient females (uteri characterized as large and flaccid, and containing red blood cells in the lumen), and by the occurrence of many females simultaneously lactating and pregnant. Female *Myotis nigricans* do not copulate for some time after parturition. Few females were found to be both lactating and pregnant, while many were lactating and showed no signs of having mated. *Lasiurus ega* females breed only once a year, so there is no opportunity for a post partum estrus.

Post partum estruses have been found in a few other species of bats: *Rousettus aegyptiacus* (Pteropidae), Mutere, 1968; *Nycteris luteola* (Nycteridae), Matthews, 1939; *Artibeus lituratus* (Phyllostomatidae), Tamsitt and Valdivieso, 1963; and *Myotis nigricans* (Vespertilionidae), Wilson, 1971.

Age at First Breeding

The most reliable estimates of the age at first breeding concern *M. nigricans*. One young female carried an unimplanted blastocyst, while others contained spermatozoa in their uteri and enlarged follicles in their ovaries. Similarly, one young male contained spermatozoa in its epididymides, and testes of other young males contained spermatids and numerous meiotic configurations. Thus both males and females reach sexual maturity by approximately four months of age in Paraguay, the same age reported for *M. nigricans* in Panama (Wilson and Findley, 1971).

While no recognizably young female *M. albescens* were pregnant, three young females captured in December had spermatozoa in their uteri and enlarged follicles in their ovaries. They were less than two months old. Young males had numerous cells in meiosis but no spermatids or spermatozoa in their testes. All males caught in winter (N=29) had testes of adult size, and all females caught in August and September (N=32, including females diagnosed only by palpation) were pregnant. Thus both sexes breed before the end of their first year, and possibly as early as two months in the case of some females born in the spring.

Similarly, both sexes of *Eptesicus* and *Lasiurus* breed before they are one year old. All male *Eptesicus* captured in April-June and September-October (N=21), and all male *Lasiurus* captured in March-July (N=15) had enlarged testes, and all whose testes were sectioned contained spermatozoa in their epididymides. All female *Eptesicus* (N=21) and *Lasiurus* (N=23) captured in early spring were pregnant.

The age of first breeding by temperate region bats varies from species to species. Most females breed in their second year, and most males breed during their first winter (Asdell, 1964). However, some females breed in their first year (*e.g., Myotis velifer*; Kunz, 1973), while males of several species do not breed until their second year or later (*e.g., Miniopterus schreibersi*; Dwyer, 1963a).

Population Structure

Individuals of *Myotis* breed at a relatively young age in Paraguay and have more litters per year than north temperate bats. This implies that populations are expanding and/or mortality rates are higher in Paraguay than in the North Temperate Zone. The two species of *Myotis* are strongly dependent on human habitations for roosts in Paraguay. Both species were invariably found in association with human constructions. Further man-made ponds are the only source of standing fresh water in large areas of the Chaco. The Indians of western Paraguay are nomadic hunters who build no permanent structures. Thus only white men have affected *Myotis* populations, and their influence is at most of a few hundred years' duration. As the number of dwellings and cattle ponds increases, the *Myotis* population would be expected to expand. Predation on bats may also be significantly greater in the Neotropics in general than in the Nearctic Region. Several tropical species of birds and large phyllostomatid bats prey on small bats. Snakes, spiders, cockroaches, and terrestrial mammalian carnivores also take a toll (Wilson, 1971). Humans are also a significant predator, particularly in the Chaco, due to the dependence of bats on man for roosting sites. Bats are killed by man and their roosts destroyed because of their smell and litter, and because of the fear of the bats serving as a vector of rabies. Finally, the low predictability of changes in insect populations may cause significant mortality. Therefore, the high reproductive rate of Paraguayan *Myotis* populations is probably associated with an increased mortality due to predation, and with population expansion due to an increase in the number of roosts.

If populations are expanding, or predation on adults is higher in the Neotropics, the age distribution of the populations should be significantly shifted toward younger ages. This hypothesis could be tested, though it would require data gathered over several additional years. North temperate bats are long-lived compared to other small mammals. There are records of wild *Eptesicus fuscus* 17+ years old (Goering, 1972); *Myotis lucifugus* lives up to 24 years (Griffin and Hitchcock, 1965); and *Pipistrellus subflavus* individuals have survived 13 years (Davis, 1966). Furthermore, several authors have calculated life table statistics for bats (*e.g.*, Pearson *et al.*, 1952; Sluiter *et al.*, 1956; Davis, 1966; Goering, 1972), so a comparison with north temperate populations would be possible. The only records for vespertilionids from the Neotropics are for *M. nigricans* in Panama (Wilson, 1971; Wilson and Tyson, 1970). In these studies, 1.5% of a population of 600 marked *Myotis* were alive after 7 years.

Wilson (1971) concluded that the dependence of *M. nigricans* on human habitations derives from its inability to compete for more natural roost sites. This, he hypothesized, might reflect a recent invasion of the tropics. However, the pattern of continual spermatogenesis and nearly continual breeding contradicts this, at least with respect to the other vespertilionids studied here. *M. nigricans* has altered the temperate breeding pattern of its ancestors more profoundly than the other species examined, perhaps suggesting a longer history in tropical environments.

Social Aggregations

Harems have been reported for colonies of *Myotis adversus* in Australia (Dwyer, 1970a). Medway (1971) reported groups of *Miniopterus australis* in caves in Borneo, with sex ratios strongly suggesting harems. Wilson (1971) notes that large groups of *Myotis nigricans* were composed largely of females (88%), while solitary animals were primarily males (81%). The roost he studied, in an attic, appeared to be intermediate in structure between the Paraguayan roosts in palm log roofs and in buildings. North temperate vespertilionids roost either solitarily (*e.g.*, lasiurines), or in small to very large colonies. During the summer all-female nursery colonies are formed, and males roost solitarily or in small groups elsewhere. During the winter large colonies, composed of both sexes, gather in caves or other hibernacula.

Comparisons of Reproductive Patterns

Lasiurus ega. – In Paraguay, the pattern of this species (one breeding period per year, insemination several months before conception, spermatogenesis in the late summer and fall, accessory glands remain large after interstitial tissue involutes) resembles the pattern of north temperate bats more closely than any of the other Paraguayan species examined. It differs primarily in the absence of hibernation. Little information is available concerning the reproduction of north temperate members of the genus *Lasiurus*. *L. borealis* and *L. cinereus* in the United States combine the storage of spermatozoa with migration and hibernation (Asdell, 1964; Barbour and Davis, 1969; Whitaker and Mumford, 1972), though they may be active on warm days during the winter (Davis and Lidicker, 1956). The genus is widespread in the American tropics and offers an excellent opportunity for further comparative study.

Eptesicus furinalis. – The closest relative of this species in the United States is *Eptesicus fuscus*. *E. fuscus* breeds once annually, and its pattern is similar to that of other north temperate vespertilionids (see Wimsatt, 1942, 1944, 1945; Christian, 1956; Phillips, 1966; Kunz, 1974). The post partum breeding found in the Paraguayan species is unknown in North America, where *E. fuscus* further differs in that hibernation intervenes between the initial insemination and ovulation.

The reproduction of *E. furinalis* in Paraguay resembles that of *E. fuscus* in that some of the embryos conceived in the first breeding period are lost between fertilization and parturition (table 3). Shortly after ovulation, the number of fertilized ova or blastocysts in the tubules or uterus approximately equals the number of corpora lutea. As gestation proceeds, embryos are lost, and the difference between the number of embryos and the number of corpora lutea grows. By late pregnancy an average of 1.9 embryos remains, while there are 3.5 corpora lutea. The data in table 3 indicate that most losses occur after implantation. In an environment that fluctuates unpredictably, this pattern may insure that the maximum number of young are raised. In an unfavorable year, some embryos can be resorbed, while in a good year, they can be brought to term. In North America, female *E. fuscus* ovulate an average of 4.24 ova each year but give birth to only one or two young (Wimsatt, 1945). Kunz (1974), reviewing the literature on *E. fuscus*, documents geographic variability in litter size. This variability is presumably in response to differing environmental conditions. Unfortunately, most studies are too short in duration to determine whether litter size changes from year to year in the same population.

The pattern in Paraguay is complicated by the second breeding season. In contrast to the first, a single embryo is invariably accompanied by a single corpus luteum.

Myotis albescens. – In Paraguay female *Myotis albescens* breed either two or three times annually and produce one young per pregnancy (fig. 12). Females may store spermatozoa, but do not hibernate. Parturition takes place in spring and summer, and breeding halts in fall and early winter. Spermatogenesis occurs during fall, winter, and spring, and spermatozoa are present in the epididymides at these times (fig. 13). The accessory glands are large when the interstitial tissue appears most active.

In temperate North America and Europe, members of the genus *Myotis* hibernate, with females and males storing spermatozoa during winter. Parturition occurs in spring or early summer, and one young per female is born each year (see Asdell, 1964; and Carter, 1970). In south-temperate Australia, Dwyer (1970b) has found that *Myotis adversus* has three breeding seasons at 22°S latitude, but two at 27°S latitude. Neither storage of spermatozoa nor developmental delays were observed. Subtropical populations of *Myotis austroriparius* have been studied in Florida (Rice, 1957; McNab, 1974). Populations in northern Florida hibernate and store spermatozoa, but those in the central part of the state do not hibernate, spermatozoa are not stored, and mating occurs in the spring. Thus, some species of *Myotis* have the ability to alter their breeding patterns as conditions change. Yet individuals of *Myotis austroriparius* in central Florida migrate northward, reportedly to permit hibernation (and storage of spermatozoa?) (McNab, 1974), suggesting that in some species this behavior is obligatory. One study exists of a tropical population of *Myotis nigricans* (see below). While there are no intensive investigations of breeding of *Myotis albescens* in the tropics, Wilson (1970) found that six male *Myotis albescens* from Amazonian Peru and from Panama had large testes and "massive sperm storage" by males (p. 56). The males thus resemble *M. albescens* in Paraguay, and are more similar to populations of *Myotis* in the temperate zone than to *M. nigricans*.

Myotis nigricans. – Breeding by females of this species in Paraguay resembles that of *M. albescens*, but probably continues at a low frequency during the fall and winter (fig. 14). The males are nearly aseasonal in their testis cycles (fig. 15); only the accessory glands change seasonally, and those changes might not be functionally important. Thus, Paraguayan populations of *M. nigricans* seem to have changed more than the other three species in the direction expected for animals living in a less seasonal, tropical environment, and their pattern of reproduction differs substantially from that of temperate zone *Myotis*.

In Panama, Wilson (1970, 1971), and Wilson and Findley (1970, 1971) found that *M. nigricans* breed in a pattern closely resembling the Paraguayan one. Females breed continually during most of the year, with a period of two to three months when reproductive activity is reduced. The decrease in breeding is thought to be related to changes in abundance of insects. Each female breeds about three times annually. Testis size changes only slightly, though spermatogenesis slows or ceases for a three month period. Wilson and Findley (1971) also examined six specimens of this species captured in Mexico. Spermatogenesis was absent, yet the epididymides were swollen with spermatozoa. The male breeding pattern of Mexican *M. nigricans* thus resembles that of North American *Myotis* more closely than that of Panamanian or Paraguayan populations of the same species.

SUMMARY

1. Females of four species of vespertilionid bats in Paraguay, *Lasiurus ega, Eptesicus furinalis, Myotis albescens,* and *M. nigricans*, give birth in the southern spring (September-November). *Eptesicus* females experience a post partum estrus and breed once more. *Myotis albescens* females probably experience a post partum estrus and breed either one or two more times. *Myotis nigricans* also breed one or two more times but without a post partum estrus; and the data suggest that there is a low level of breeding by *Myotis nigricans* throughout the year. The breeding schedule of all four species results in the birth of fewer young in late fall and winter than in other seasons.

2. The relationship of the male cycles of the four species is complex. The epididymides of all four species contain spermatozoa in late fall and late winter, but the pattern of each species is distinct. *Myotis nigricans* is unique in that spermatozoa are present throughout the year. The hiatus in spermatogenesis during the summer in the other three species may be related to high temperatures in that season.

3. Female *Lasiurus ega, Eptesicus furinalis,* and *Myotis albescens* copulate 1 to 3 months before they become pregnant in the spring, suggesting that these species resemble north temperate vespertilionid populations in that females store spermatozoa. Females were not isolated from males after they first bred, and so the possibility remains that spermatozoa from early copulations are quickly lost and replaced by subsequent matings.

4. Paraguayan bats do not hibernate, though daily torpor is important in cool seasons.

5. The relationship between interstitial tissue, accessory glands, and spermatogenesis is described. In *Lasiurus ega* males, the interstitial tissue appears to involute more than a month in advance of the accessory glands. In *Myotis albescens* and *Eptesicus furinalis*, the interstitial tissue and accessory glands appear to change together. The relationship between these patterns and those of north temperate vespertilionids is discussed.

6. All four species first breed when less than one year old. *Myotis nigricans* females are capable of becoming pregnant at 3 to 4 months. Paraguayan populations of *Myotis* breed at a younger age, and more often each year than north temperate populations. This probably implies either greater mortality of Paraguayan bats, or expanding populations, or both.

7. *Myotis nigricans* males and females appear to segregate into harems under some conditions. These harems are remarkably cohesive in membership and are not attached to a particular site.

ACKNOWLEDGMENTS

Many people assisted in this study, and it would be impossible to acknowledge all of them. However, in Berkeley, J. L. Patton and O. P. Pearson, co-chairmen of my thesis committee, and my wife, Lora, provided advice, assistance, and encouragement, without which the study would never have been completed. Financial assistance from the Museum of Vertebrate Zoology, University of California, Berkeley, is gratefully acknowledged. In the Paraguayan Chaco, Oscar Netto, Robert Eaton, and Ernesto Weiler allowed us to stay at their ranches for extended periods, and Ralph M. Wetzel and Robert Martin provided advice and encouragement in the field. In Asunción, my parents, Mr. and Mrs. Philip Myers, provided a base of operations at their home and the most productive swimming pool in Asunción (from the point of view of netting bats). Officials of the Ministério de Agricultura y Ganaderia permitted us to work at an agricultural experimental station in the Chaco, and expedited permits for the export of scientific specimens.

I also thank John Davis and Robert Ornduff, University of California, Berkeley, for their criticisms of this paper. The figures were prepared by Emily Reid, Lora Myers, and Mark Orsen.

LITERATURE CITED

ADAMOLI, J., R. NEUMANN, A. D. RATIER DE COLINA, y J. MORELLO
    1972. El Chaco aluvional salteño. Rev. Invest. Agropecu. Ser. 3, Clima Suelo, 9(5):165-237.

ANDERSON, J. W., and W. A. WIMSATT
    1963. Placentation and fetal membranes of the Central American noctilionid bat *Noctilio labialis minor.* Am. J. Anat., 112:181-199.

ASDELL, S. A.
    1964. Patterns of mammalian reproduction. Ithaca: Cornell University Press, xi + 670 pp.

BAKER, J. R., and T. F. BIRD
    1936. The seasons in a tropical rain forest (New Hebrides). Part 4. Insectivorous bats (Vespertilionidae and Rhinolophidae). J. Linn. Soc. Lond. Zool., 40(269):143-161.

BARBOUR, R. W., and W. H. DAVIS
    1969. Bats of America. Lexington: The University Press of Kentucky, 286 pp.

BERTONI, G. T., and J. R. GORHAM
    1973. The geography of Paraguay. *In* J. R. Gorham, ed., Paraguay: ecological essays. Miami: Academy of Arts and Sciences of the Americas. Pp. 9-31.

BLEIER, W. J.
    1975. Crystalline structure in the ova and early embryological stages in a leaf-nosed bat, *Macrotus californicus.* J. Mammal., 56(1):235-238.

BONACCORSO, F. J., and N. SMYTHE
    1972. Punch-marking bats: an alternative to banding. J. Mammal., 53(2):389-390.

BRADSHAW, G. V. R.
    1962. Reproductive cycle of the California leaf-nosed bat, *Macrotus californicus.* Science, 136:645.

CABRERA, A.
    1957. Catálogo de los mamiferos de América del Sur I. (Metatheria-Unguiculata-Carnivora). Rev. Mus. Argent. Cienc. Nat. 'Bernardino Rivadavia' Inst. Nat. Invest. Cienc. Nat. B. Aires Cienc. Zool., 4(1):1-307.

CARTER, D. C.
    1970. Chiropteran reproduction. *In* B. H. Slaughter and D. W. Walton, eds., About bats. Dallas: Southern Methodist University Press. Pp. 233-246.

CHRISTIAN, J. J.
    1956. The natural history of a summer aggregation of *Eptesicus fuscus fuscus.* Amer. Midl. Nat., 55(1):66-95.

COURRIER, R.
    1927. Etude sur le déterminisme des caractères sexuel secondaires chez quelque mammifères à activité testiculaire périodique. Arch. Biol., 37:173-334.

DAVIS, W. H.
    1966. Population dynamics of the bat *Pipistrellus subflavus.* J. Mammal., 47(3):383-396.

DAVIS, W. H., and W. Z. LIDICKER, JR.
    1956. Winter range of the red bat, *Lasiurus borealis.* J. Mammal., 37(2):280-281.

DWYER, P. D.
    1963a. The breeding biology of *Miniopterus Schreibersii blepotis* (Temminck) (Chiroptera) in northeastern New South Wales. Aust. J. Zool., 11:219-240.
    1963b. Reproduction and distribution in *Miniopterus* (Chiroptera). Aust. J. Sci., 25:435-436.
    1968. The biology, origin, and adaptations of *Miniopterus australis* (Chiroptera) in New South Wales. Aust. J. Zool., 16:49-68.
    1970a. Social organization in the bat *Myotis adversus.* Science, 168:1006-1008.
    1970b. Latitude and breeding season in a polyestrus species of *Myotis.* J. Mammal, 51(2):405-410.
    1971. Temperature regulation and cave-dwelling in bats: an evolutionary perspective. Mammalia, 35(3):424-455.

FLEMING, T. H.
    1971. *Artibeus jamaicensis:* delayed embryonic development in a neotropical bat. Science, 171:402-404.

FLEMING, T. H., E. T. HOOPER, and D. E. WILSON
  1972. Three Central American bat communities: structure, reproductive cycles, and movement patterns. Ecology, 53(4):553-569.
GLOVER, T. D., and D. H. YOUNG
  1963. Temperature and the production of spermatozoa. Fertil. and Steril., 14(4):441-450.
GOERING, H. H.
  1972. Twenty-year study of *Eptesicus fuscus* in Minnesota. J. Mammal., 53(1):201-207.
GOPALAKRISHNA, A.
  1947. Studies on the embryology of Microchiroptera. Part I. Reproduction and breeding seasons in the South Indian vespertilionid bat – *Scotophilus wroughtoni* (Thomas). Proc. Indian Acad. Sci., Sec. B, 26:219-232.
GORHAM, J. R.
  1973. The Paraguayan Chaco and its rainfall. *In* J. R. Gorham, ed., Paraguay: ecological essays. Miami: Academy of Arts and Sciences of the Americas. Pp. 39-60.
GRIFFIN, D. R.
  1970. Migrations and homing of bats. *In* W. A. Wimsatt, ed., Biology of bats, Vol. II. New York and London: Academic Press. Pp. 233-264.
GRIFFIN, D. R., and H. B. HITCHCOCK
  1965. Probable 24-year longevity records for *Myotis lucifugus*. J. Mammal., 46(2):332.
GUTHRIE, M. J.
  1933. The reproductive cycle of some cave bats. J. Mammal., 14(3):199-216.
HALL, E. R., and K. R. KELSON
  1959. The mammals of North America. New York: Ronald Press. xxx + 1083 pp. (2 vols.)
KOOPMAN, K. F.
  1970. Zoogeography of bats. *In* B. H. Slaughter and D. W. Walton, eds., About bats. Dallas: Southern Methodist University Press. Pp. 29-50.
KRUTZSCH, P. H.
  1956. The reproductive cycle in the male bat of the species *Pipistrellus hesperus*. Anat. Rec., 124(2):321-322.
KUNZ, T. H.
  1973. Population studies of the cave bat (*Myotis velifer*): reproduction, growth, and development. Occas. Pap. Mus. Nat. Hist. Univ. Kans., 15:1-43.
  1974. Reproduction, growth, and mortality of the vespertilionid bat, *Eptesicus fuscus*, in Kansas. J. Mammal., 55(1):1-13.
LAVAL, R. K.
  1973. A revision of the neotropical bats of the genus *Myotis*. Bull. Nat. Hist. Mus., L. A. Co. Mus. Sci., 15:1-54.
LIDICKER, W. Z., JR.
  1973. Regulation of numbers in an island population of the California vole, a problem in community dynamics. Ecol. Monogr., 43:271-302.
MARSHALL, A. J., and P. S. CORBET
  1959. The breeding biology of equatorial vertebrates: reproduction of the bat *Chaerophon hindei* Thomas at latitude 0°26′N. Proc. Zool. Soc. Lond., 132:607-616.
MATTHEWS, L. H.
  1939. Post-partum oestrus in a bat. Nature (Lond.), 143:643.
MCNAB, B. K.
  1969. The economics of temperature regulation in neotropical bats. Comp. Biochem. Physiol., 31:227-268.
  1974. The behavior of temperate cave bats in a subtropical environment. Ecology, 55:943-958.
MEDWAY, LORD
  1971. Observations of social and reproductive biology of the bent-winged bat *Miniopterus australis* in northern Borneo. J. Zool., Lond., 165:261-273.
MILLER, R. E.
  1939. The reproductive cycle in male bats of the species *Myotis lucifugus lucifugus* and *Myotis grisescens*. J. Morphol., 64(2):267-295.

MITCHELL, G. C.
    1965. A natural history study of the funnel-eared bat, *Natalus stramineus*. M.A. thesis, Univ. of Arizona.

MOSSMAN, H. W., and K. L. DUKE
    1973. Comparative morphology of the mammalian ovary. Madison: University of Wisconsin Press, xxviii + 461 pp.

MUTERE, F. A.
    1967. The breeding biology of equatorial vertebrates: reproduction in the fruit bat, *Eidolon helvum* Kerr at latitude 0°20'N. J. Zool., Proc. Zool. Soc. Lond., 153:153-161.
    1968. The breeding biology of the fruit bat *Rousettus aegyptiacus* E. Geoffroy living at 0°22'S. Acta Trop., 25(2):97-108.
    1973. A comparative study of reproduction in two populations of the insectivorous bats, *Otomops martiensseni*, at latitudes 1°5'S and 2°30'S. J. Zool., Lond., 171:79-92.

ORR, R. T.
    1954. Natural history of the pallid bat, *Antrozous pallidus* (LeConte). Proc. Calif. Acad. Sci., 28(4):165-246.

PAGENSTECHER, H. A.
    1859. Ueber die Begattung von *Vesperugo pipistrellus*. Verh. des Naturhist-mediz. Vereins zu Heidelberg, i, p. 194.

PEARSON, O. P., M. R. KOFORD, and A. K. PEARSON
    1952. Reproduction of the lump-nosed bat (*Corynorhinus rafinesquei*) in California. J. Mammal., 33(3):273-320.

PEYRE, A., and M. HERLANT
    1963. Correlations hypophysogénitales chez la femelle du Minioptère (*Miniopterus schreibersii* B.). Gen. Comp. Endocrinol., 3(6):726-727.

PHILLIPS, G. L.
    1966. Ecology of the big brown bat (Chiroptera: Vespertilionidae) in northeastern Kansas. Amer. Midl. Nat., 75:168-198.

PLANEL, H., A. GUILHEM, and J. P. SOLEILHAUOUP
    1962. Le cycle annuel du cortex surrenal d'un semi-hibernant: *Miniopterus schreibersii*. C. R. Assoc. Anat., 113:620-633.

RACEY, P. A.
    1973. Environmental factors affecting the length of gestation in heterothermic bats. J. Reprod. Fertil., Suppl., 19:175-189.

RACEY, P. A., and W. H. TAM
    1974. Reproduction in male *Pipistrellus pipistrellus* (Mammalia: Chiroptera). J. Zool., Lond., 172:101-122.

RICE, D. W.
    1957. Life history and ecology of *Myotis austroriparius* in Florida. J. Mammal., 38(1):15-32.

SANCHEZ, T. F.
    1973. The climate of Paraguay. In J. R. Gorham, ed., Paraguay: ecological essays. Miami: Academy of Arts and Sciences of the Americas. Pp. 33-38.

SHORT, L. L.
    1975. A zoogeographic analysis of the South American Chaco avifauna. Bull. Amer. Mus. Nat. Hist., 154(3):163-352.

SLUITER, J. W., and M. BOWMAN
    1951. Sexual maturity in bats of the genus *Myotis*. I. Size and histology of the reproductive organs during hibernation in connection with age and wear of the teeth in female *Myotis myotis* and *M. emarginatus*. Proc. K. Ned. Akad. Wet., Ser. C Biol. Med. Sci., 54:594-602.

SLUITER, J. W., P. F. VAN HEERDT, and J. J. BEZEM
    1956. Population statistics of the bat *Myotis mystacinus*, based on the marking-recapture method. Arch. Neerl. Zool., 7:63-88.

TAMSITT, J. R., and D. VALDIVIESO
    1963. Reproductive cycle of the big fruit-eating bat, *Artibeus lituratus* Olfers. Nature (Lond.), 198(4875):104.

1965a. The male reproductive cycle of the bat *Artibeus lituratus*. Amer. Midl. Nat., 73(1):150-160.

1965b. Reproduction of the female big fruit-eating bat, *Artibeus lituratus palmarum*, in Colombia. Caribb. J. Sci., 5:157-166.

TAYLOR, L. R.
    1963. Analysis of the effect of temperature on insects in flight. J. Anim. Ecol., 32:99-117.

TUTTLE, M. D.
    1975. Population ecology of the gray bat (*Myotis grisescens*): factors influencing early growth and development. Occ. Pap. Mus. Nat. Hist. Univ. Kans., 36:1-24.

WAITES, G. M. H. and B. P. SETCHELL
    1969. Some physiological aspects of the function of the testis. *In* K. W. McKerns, ed., The gonads. New York: Appleton-Century-Crofts. Pp. 649-714.

WEIBEL, E. R., G. S. KISTLER, and W. F. SCHERLE
    1966. Practical stereological methods for morphometric cytology. J. Cell. Biol., 30:23-38.

WETZEL, R. M., and J. W. LOVETT
    1974. A collection of mammals from the Chaco of Paraguay. Occ. Pap. Univ. Conn., 2(13):203-216.

WHITAKER, J. O., JR., and R. E. MUMFORD
    1972. Notes on occurrence and reproduction of bats in Indiana. Proc. Indiana Acad. Sci. (1971), 81(1972):376-383.

WILSON, D. E.
    1970. Life history of *Myotis nigricans* (Mammalia: Chiroptera). Ph.D thesis, University of New Mexico. Ann Arbor: University Microfilms, 94 pp.

    1971. Ecology of *Myotis nigricans* (Mammalia: Chiroptera) on Barro Colorado Island, Panama Canal Zone. J. Zool., Proc. Zool. Soc. Lond., 163(1):1-13.

WILSON, D. E., and J. S. FINDLEY
    1970. Reproductive cycle of a neotropical insectivorous bat, *Myotis nigricans*. Nature, 225(5238):1155.

    1971. Spermatogenesis in some neotropical species of *Myotis*. J. Mammal., 52(2):420-426.

WILSON, D. E., and E. L. TYSON
    1970. Longevity records for *Artibeus jamaicensis* and *Myotis nigricans*. J. Mammal., 51(1):203.

WIMSATT, W. A.
    1942. Survival of spermatozoa in the female reproductive tract of the bat. Anat. Rec., 83(2):299-307.

    1944. Further studies on the survival of spermatozoa in the female reproductive tract of the bat. Anat. Rec., 88(2):193-204.

    1945. Notes on breeding behavior, pregnancy, and parturition in some vespertilionid bats of the eastern United States. J. Mammal., 26(1):23-33.

    1960. Some problems of reproduction in relation to hibernation in bats. Bull. Mus. Comp. Zool., 124:249-267.

WIMSATT, W. A. and H. TRAPIDO
    1952. Reproduction and the female reproductive cycle in the tropical American vampire bat, *Desmodus rotundus murinus*. Am. J. Anat., 91(3):415-445.

PLATES

Plate 1
a. Grassland and caranday palms (*Copernicia* sp.), Paraguayan Chaco.
b. Thorn scrub, Paraguayan Chaco.

a

b

Plate 2
a. Thorn scrub, Paraguayan Chaco.
b. Subtropical forest, Eastern Region of Paraguay.

a

b

Plate 3
a. Roof constructed of split palm logs.
b. Size and morphology of testes and epididymides of breeding males of *Myotis albescens* (left) and *M. nigricans* (right).

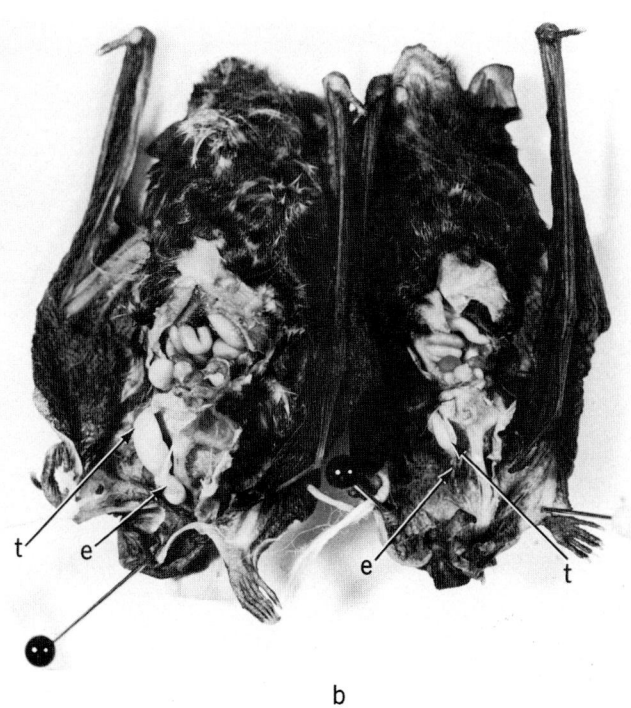

a

b

Plate 4

Ovarian morphology of adult female *Lasiurus ega* in Paraguay. (i = inclusion, mc = medullary cord, r = rete ovarii). Scale: *a-c, e-f*, line = 100 μ. *d, g-h*, line = 10 μ.

a. 29 January, developing follicles.
b. 25 May, developing follicles.
c. 17 August, large tertiary follicle (ovulation would have occurred within the next two weeks).
d. 29 January, darkly staining inclusion in ovum.
e. 25 September, corpus luteum from female with recently implanted embryo.
f. 16 October, corpus luteum from female with 19 mm embryo.
g. 25 September, same as *e*, above.
h. 16 October, same as *f*, above. Note smaller cells and shriveled appearance of nuclei compared to *g*.

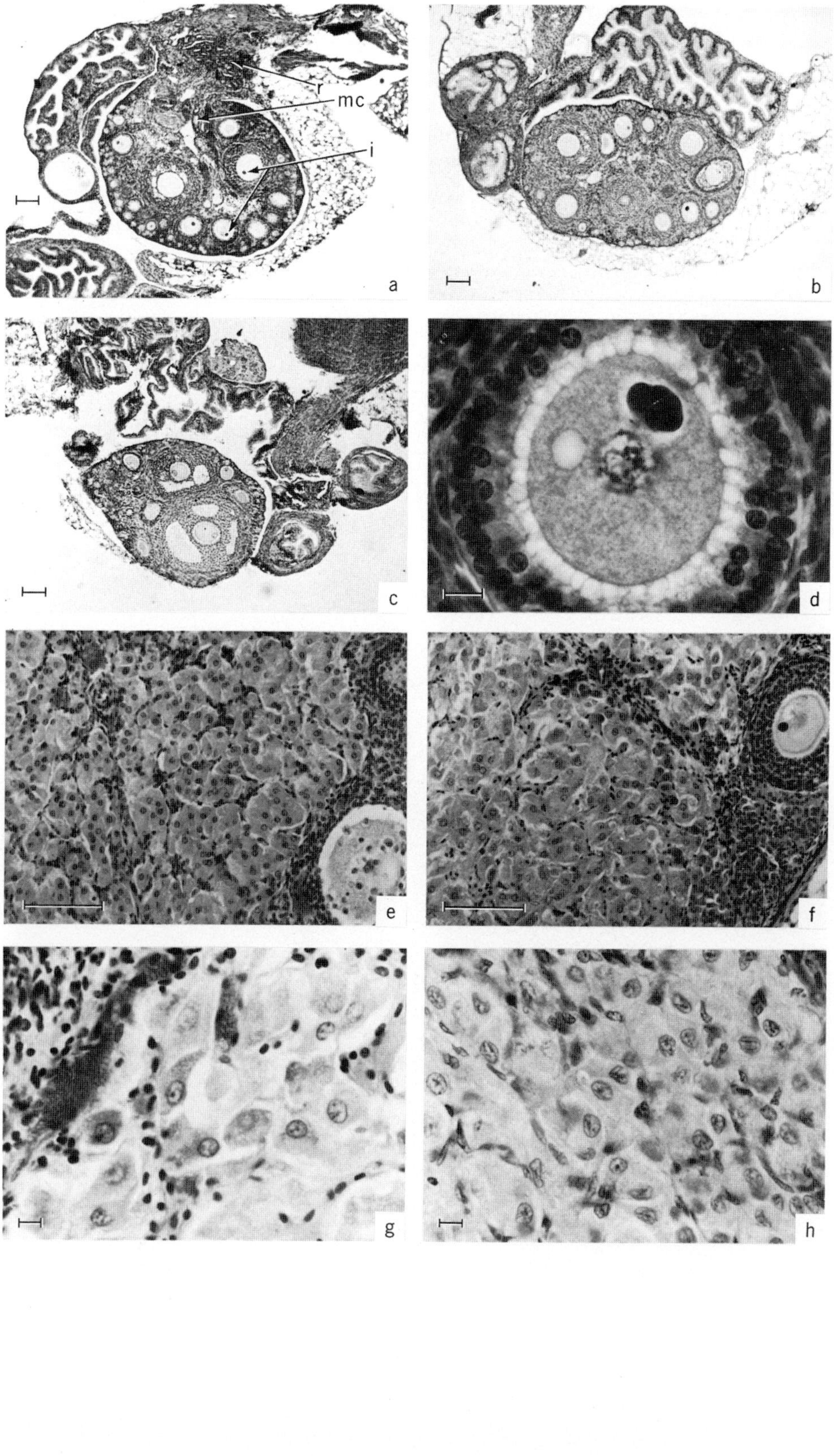
r
mc
i
a
b
c
d
e
f
g
h

Plate 5

Testicular cycle of adult male *Lasiurus ega* in Paraguay. (it = interstitial tissue). Scale: *a-d*, line = 100 μ. *e-h*, line = 50 μ.

a. 3 December, numerous cells in meiosis, no spermatids or spermatozoa.
b. 28 February, cells of all stages of spermatogenesis abundant.
c. 20 May, few cells in meiosis, spermatids and spermatozoa present.
d. 17 August, few cells in meiosis, few spermatozoa present.
e. 3 December, interstitial cells and cell nuclei small.
f. 28 February, interstitial cells large, nuclei large and rounded.
g. 20 May, interstitial cells and nuclei large but nuclei with slightly wrinkled surface.
h. 17 August, interstitial cells and cell nuclei small, surface of nuclei appears shriveled.

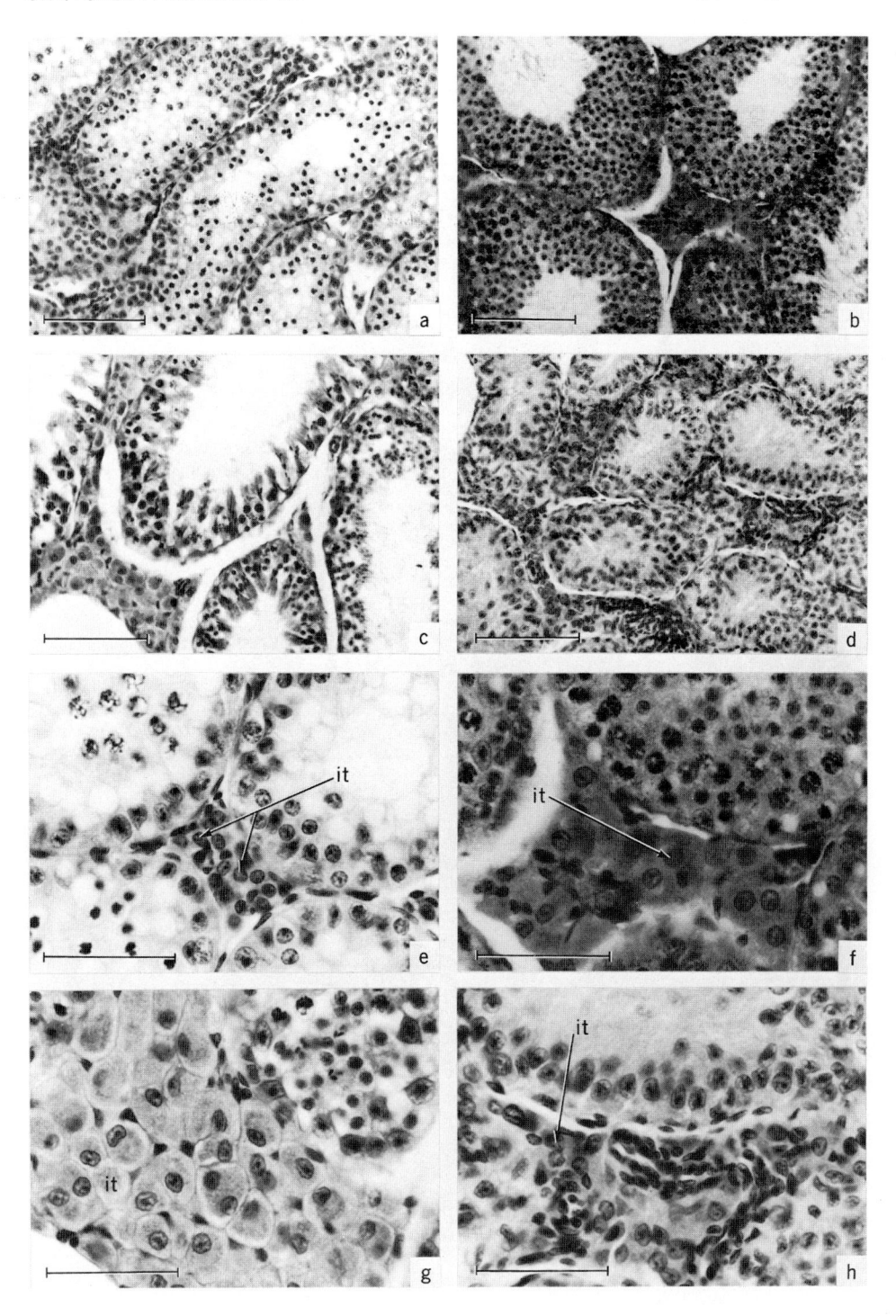
a
b
c
d
it
e
it
f
it
g
it
h

Plate 6

Ovarian morphology of adult female *Eptesicus furinalis* in Paraguay. (r = rete). Scale: *a-f*, line = 100 μ. *g-h*, line = 10 μ.

a. 4 April, developing follicles.
b. 31 May, follicles larger, but those which will ovulate not yet recognizable.
c. 7 July, large tertiary follicle, ovulation to take place in 2 to 3 weeks.
d. 9 September, three corpora lutea from female with a 9 mm embryo.
e. 30 November, corpus luteum from female with recently implanted embryo.
f. 26 October, corpus luteum from female with 22 mm embryo.
g. Same as *e*, above, note large cell nuclei and nucleoli.
h. Same as *f*, above, note smaller cell nuclei and less prominent nucleoli.

UNIV. CALIF. PUBL. ZOOL. 107 [MYERS] PLATE 6

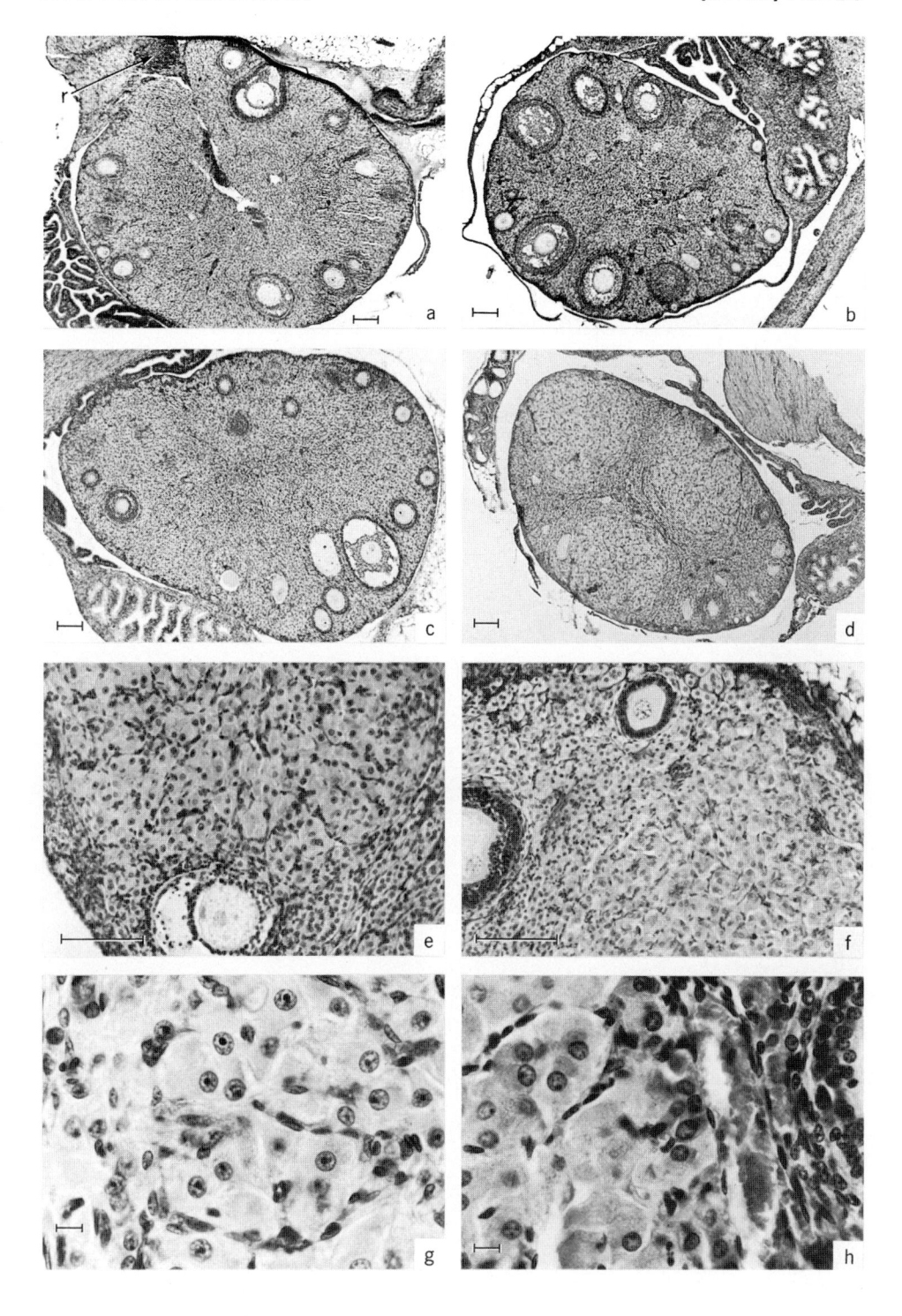

Plate 7

Testicular cycle of adult male *Eptesicus furinalis* in Paraguay. (it = interstitial tissue). Scale: *a-d*, line = 100 μ. *e-h*, line = 50 μ.

a. 8 December, numerous cells in meiosis.
b. 13 May, cells in all stages of spermatogenesis abundant.
c. 6 July, spermatids and spermatozoa only.
d. 28 September, cells in all stages of spermatogenesis abundant.
e. 8 December, interstitial cells and cell nuclei small and appear shriveled.
f. 13 May, interstitial cells and cell nuclei large, nuclei rounded.
g. 6 July, interstitial cells and cell nuclei smaller, slightly shriveled.
h. 28 September, interstitial cells and cell nuclei large and rounded.

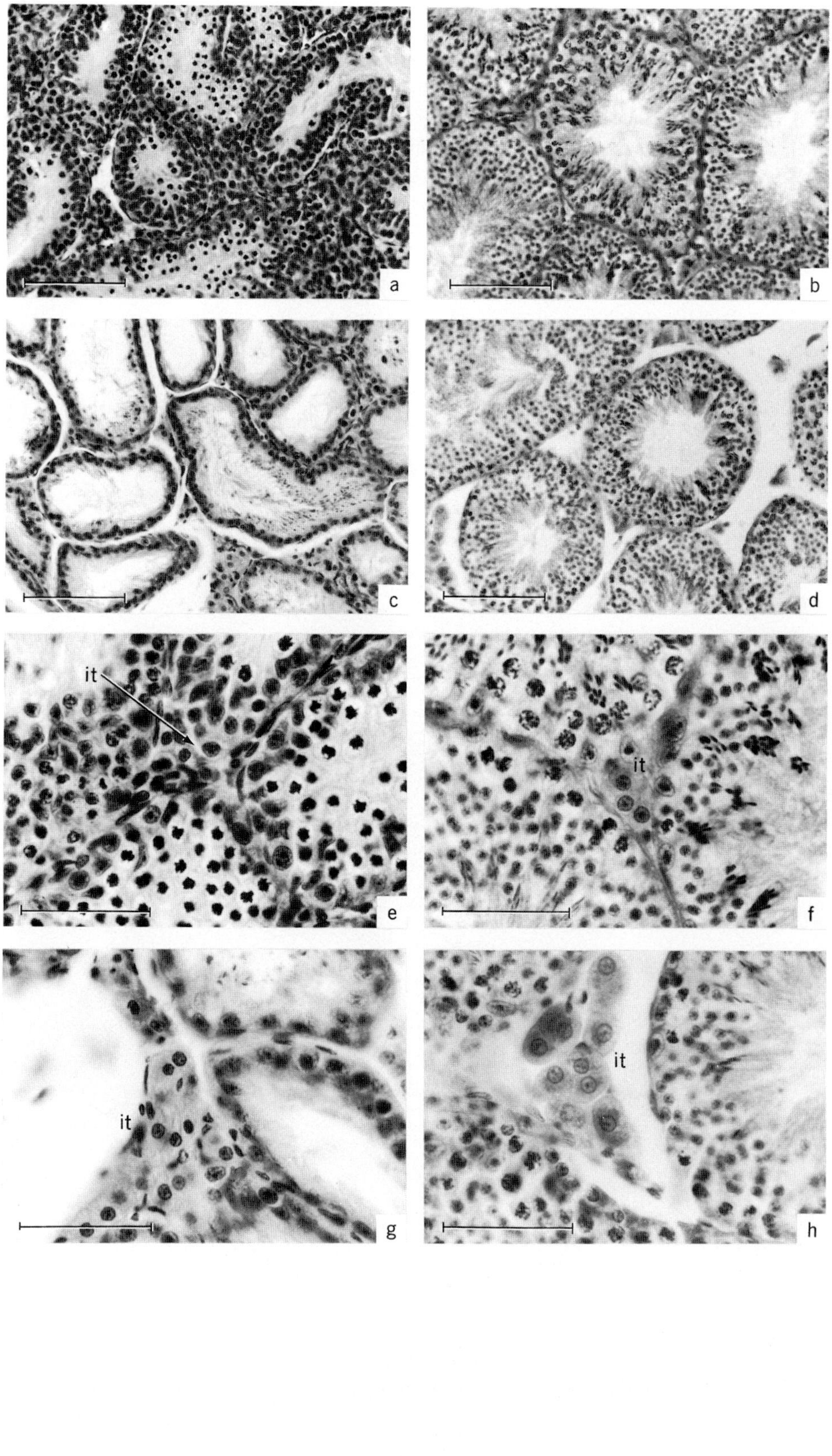
a
b
c
d
it
e
it
f
it
g
it
h

Plate 8

Ovarian morphology of adult female *Myotis albescens* in Paraguay. (mc = medullary cords, r = rete). Scale: *a-f*, line = 100 μ. *g-h*, line = 10 μ.

a. 2 April, small and medium size follicles.
b. 11 May, developing follicles.
c. 27 July, newly formed corpus luteum of female with tubal ovum.
d. 20 February, corpus luteum from female with 20 mm embryo, note small diameter and increased vascularity of corpus luteum compared to *c*.
e. Same as *c*, above, note lack of large blood vessels.
f. Same as *d*, above, note extensive vascularity.
g. Same as *c*, above, note rounded nuclei and prominent nucleoli.
h. Same as *d*, above, showing decrease in size of luteal cells and their nuclei, and less prominent nucleoli.

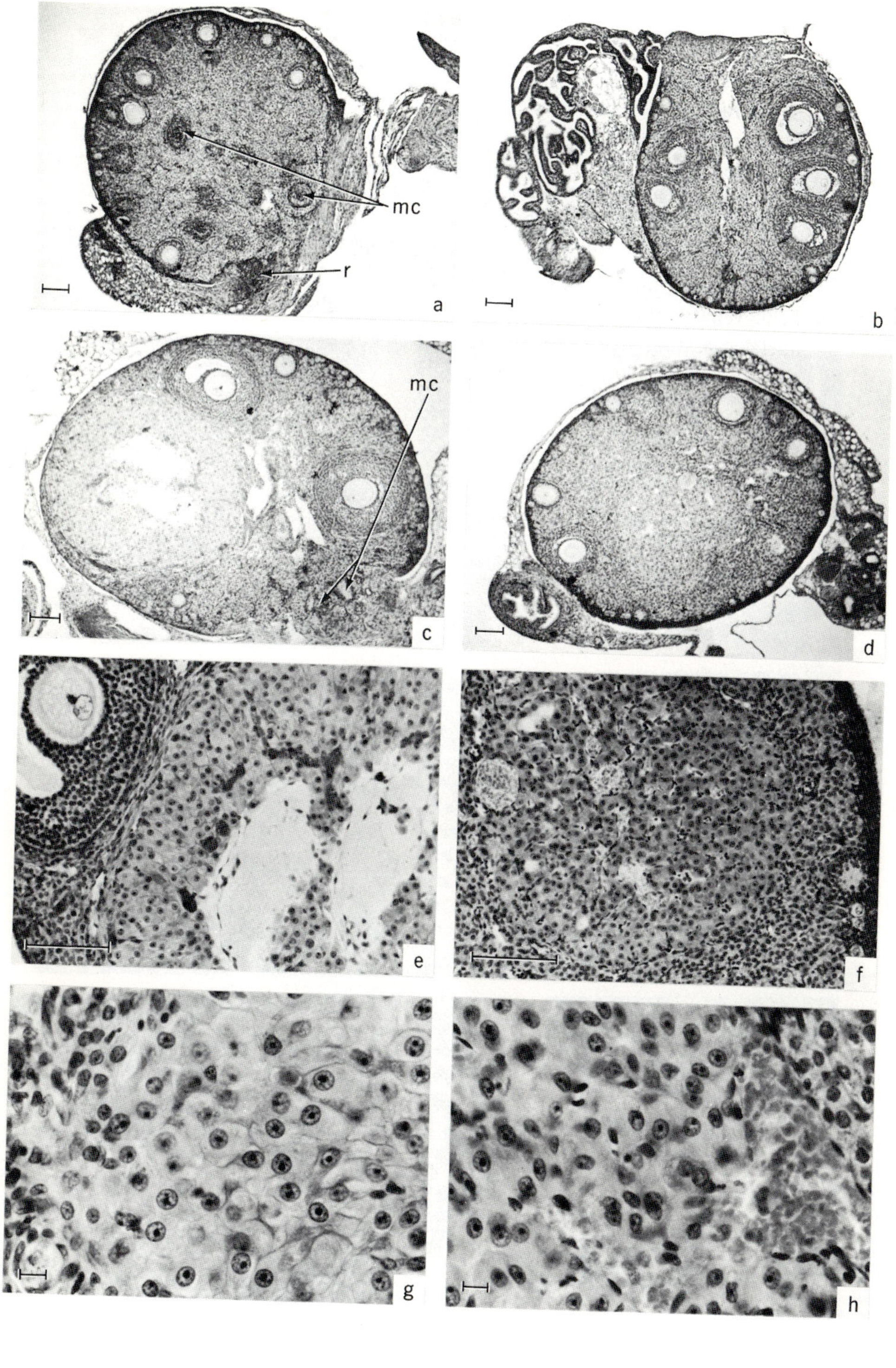
mc
r
a
b
mc
c
d
e
f
g
h

Plate 10

Ovarian morphology of adult female *Myotis nigricans* in Paraguay. (mc = medullary cord, r = rete). Scale: *a-f*, line = 100 μ. *g-h*, line = 10 μ.

a. 1 April.
b. 10 June.
c. 23 October, lactating female with many follicles in advanced stages of atresia.
d. 10 June, immature female, numerous polyovular follicles.
e. 26 July, corpus luteum from female with unimplanted embryo.
f. 21 September, corpus luteum from female with 14 mm embryo, note increased vascularity compared to *e*
g. Same as *e,* above, note large cells and cell nuclei, and prominent nucleoli.
h. Same as *f,* above, note decrease in size of cells, nuclei, and nucleoli compared to *g*.

UNIV. CALIF. PUBL. ZOOL. 107 [MYERS] PLATE 10

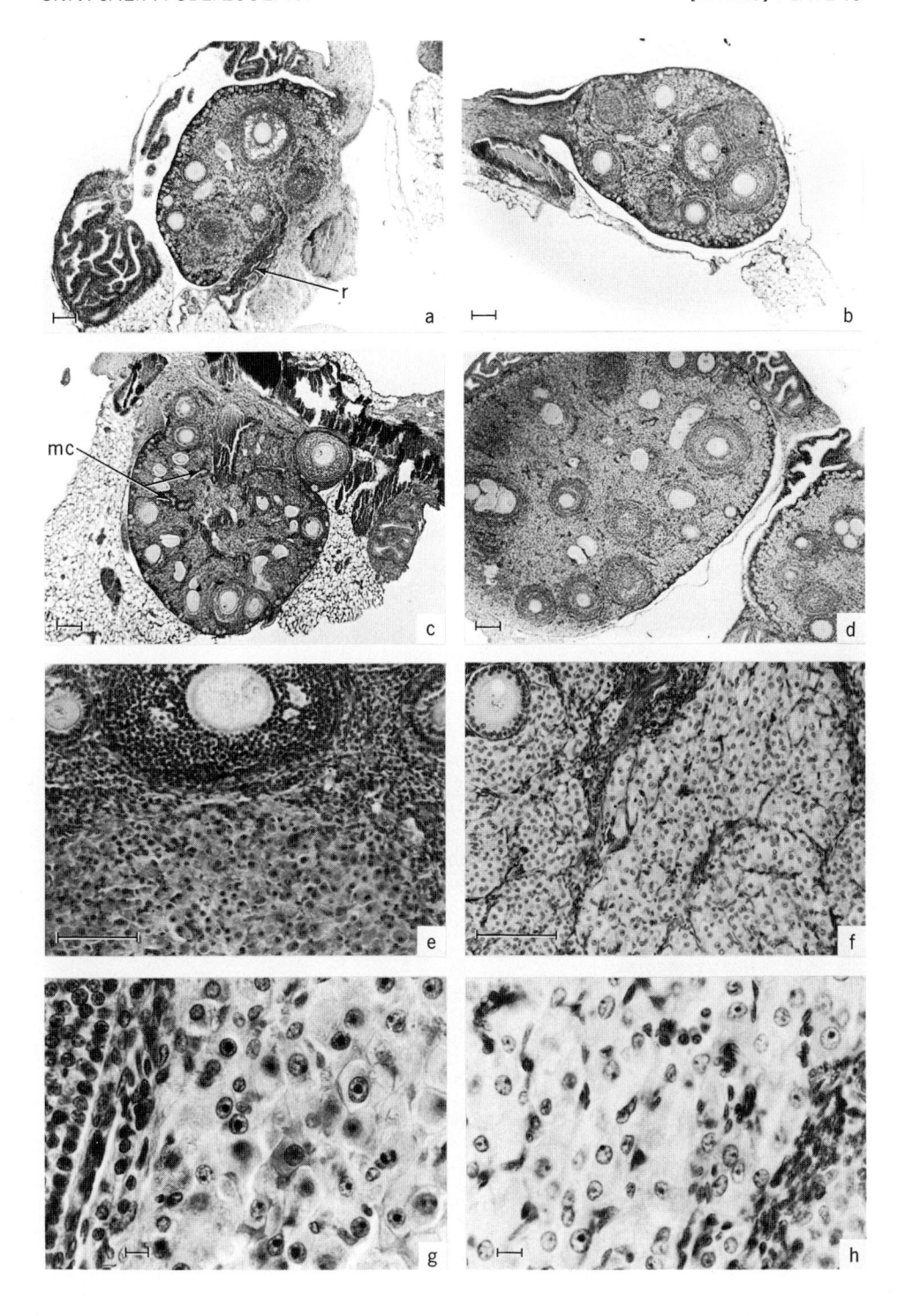

Plate 11

Testicular cycle of adult male *Myotis nigricans* in Paraguay. (it = interstitial tissue). Scale: *a-d*, line = 100 μ. *e-h*, line = 50 μ.

a. 19 February.
b. 11 May.
c. 21 September.
d. 21 November, note similarity of *a-d*.
e. 19 February.
f. 11 May.
g. 21 September.
h. 21 November, note similarity of *e-h*.

UNIV. CALIF. PUBL. ZOOL 107 [MYERS] PLATE 11

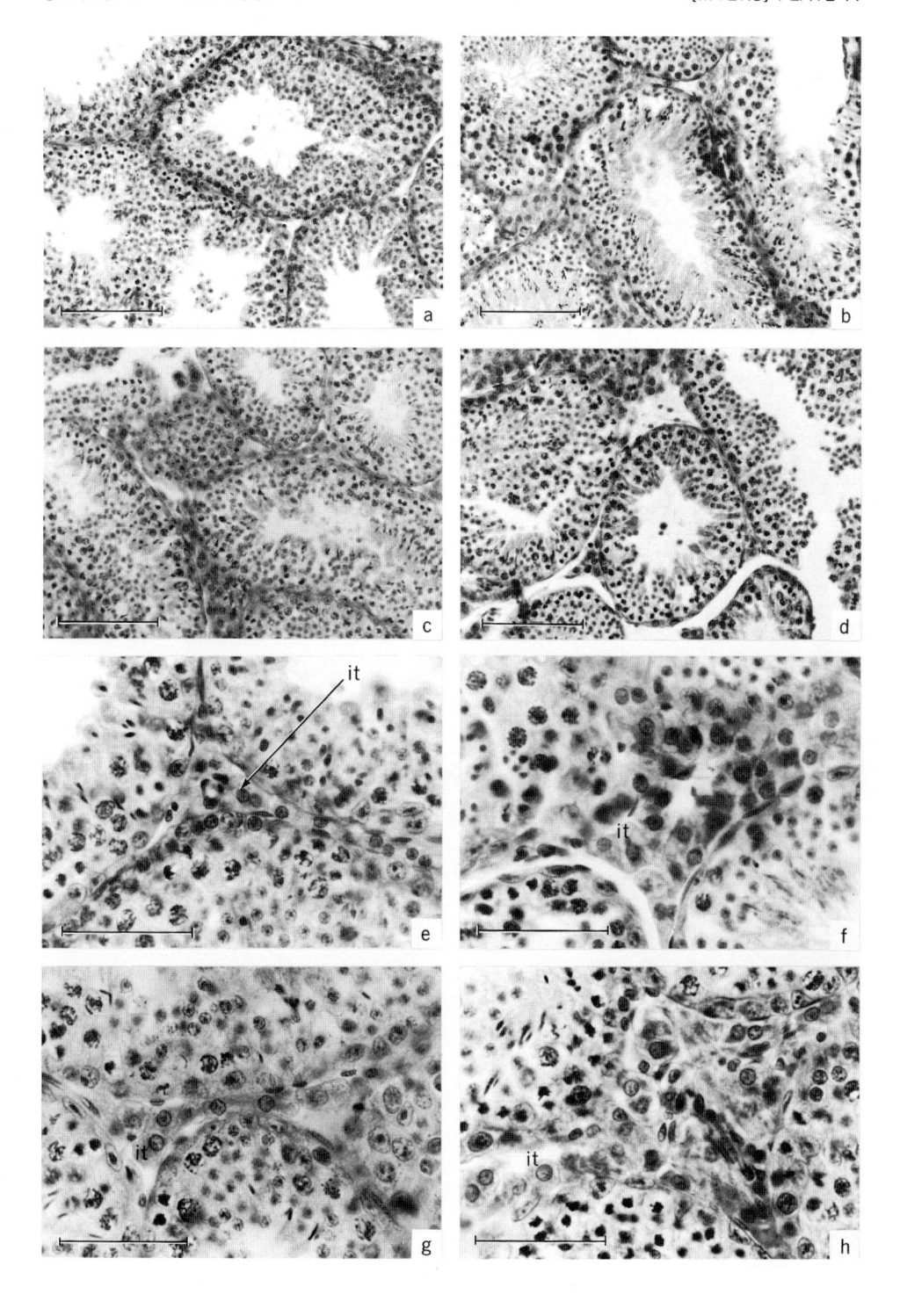